LINCOLN CHRISTIAN COLLEGE AND SEMINARY

P9-DEO-051

planning educational systems

Planning
Educational
Systems

A RESULTS-BASED APPROACH

Roger Kaufman, Ph.D.
Professor and Director
Center for Needs Assessment and Planning
The Florida State University

TECHNOMIC
PUBLISHING CO., INC.
LANCASTER · BASEL

Published in the Western Hemisphere by
Technomic Publishing Company, Inc.
851 New Holland Avenue
Box 3535
Lancaster, Pennsylvania 17604 U.S.A.

Distributed in the Rest of the World by
Technomic Publishing AG

©1988 by Technomic Publishing Company, Inc.
All rights reserved

No part of this publication may be reproduced, stored in a
retrieval system, or transmitted, in any form or by any means,
electronic, mechanical, photocopying, recording, or otherwise,
without the prior written permission of the publisher.

Printed in the United States of America
10 9 8 7 6 5 4 3 2 1

Main entry under title:
   Planning Educational Systems: A Results-Based Approach

A Technomic Publishing Company book
Bibliography: p. 203
Includes index p. 209

Library of Congress Card No. 88-50462
ISBN No. 87762-556-5

To the critically important Js in my life . . . still.

TABLE OF CONTENTS

Preface   *xi*

Acknowledgement   *xv*

Chapter 1 **Planning—An Introduction** **1**
    useful, humane results   *1*
    change   *2*
    some beginnings of educational system planning   *5*
    a holistic focus   *7*
    some definitions and basic concepts   *12*
    education, planning, and management   *18*
    summary   *21*
    glossary   *21*
    exercises   *23*

Chapter 2 **Education as a Management Process** **25**
    management, accountability, and results   *26*
    a description of the elements of a system approach to
      educational management   *28*
    defining and correctly linking the various units of
      analysis   *36*
    management of education: an interim summary   *40*
    finding the right planning level (and tools to use at the
      right place)   *41*
    getting from "what is" to "what should be"   *43*
    system analysis summary   *51*
    problem resolution   *52*
    some assumptions   *54*
    usefulness of a system approach   *55*
    summary: system analysis, system approach, and
      planning   *56*

summary: how the concepts (and tools) of a system approach
are related   *58*
glossary   *60*
exercises   *62*

Chapter 3 **Assessing Educational Needs** **63**
nine recommended steps for doing a needs assessment   *64*
using the needs data   *87*
needs assessments are practical   *87*
glossary   *88*
exercises   *89*

Chapter 4 **Mission Analysis** **91**
what is a mission?   *92*
the mission objective   *93*
the mission profile   *103*
summary   *110*
glossary   *111*
exercises   *111*

Chapter 5 **Function Analysis** **113**
levels of function analysis   *115*
the rules of function analysis   *119*
a few tips on conducting an analysis   *124*
performing a function analysis   *126*
function analysis summary and review   *133*
function analysis and feasibility   *134*
task analysis: a system analysis option   *135*
task analysis summary   *141*
glossary   *145*
exercises   *145*

Chapter 6 **Methods-Means Analysis** **149**
what is a methods-means analysis?   *149*
procedure for performing methods-means analysis   *157*
the methods-means analysis as a feasibility study   *158*
summary   *160*
glossary   *161*
exercises   *161*

Chapter 7 **Doing What You've Planned** **163**
selecting solution strategies from among alternatives   *165*
summary of selection alternatives   *170*
implementation: doing . . . at last!   *170*
determination of performance effectiveness and efficiency
(evaluation)   *171*

revised as required   *173*
summary   *173*
glossary   *174*
exercises   *175*

Chapter 8 **Applying the Models: The Gotham School District** **177**
an eighteen-step process for a system approach to
education   *201*

Bibliography   *203*

Index   *209*

About the Author   *213*

PREFACE

WHENEVER I HAVE difficulty contemplating what the next fifteen or twenty years might bring, I look back over the same time frame and note the breathtaking shifts which have occurred. It was this realization of the dynamic nature of the future and the experiences of the past that led me to what is in this book. Change is part of our reality. It always has been. Planning should help us to be masters rather than victims of change, and so too should a book on the topic help us envision and obtain a better tomorrow.

When writing this book, it was initially tempting to make a few changes to *Educational System Planning* which was written and published in the early 1970s. It provided innovative concepts which are still useful, including a needs assessment and planning orientation that focused on the learner and society. It also had a detailed discussion of the tools for educational system analysis. That book has been used for over fourteen years and was a comfortable friend. But that is the past, and now the future deserves our best attention.

As I looked back over the intervening two decades, it was an invigorating experience to realize just how much our educational world had changed. A simple book rewrite would not do. What it takes for educational planning to be responsive and responsible has changed dramatically in the last twenty years. Many lessons have been learned; we now have the opportunity to apply them to our current and future realities. By my providing here new content and understandings, I am not turning my back on the past, but using those experiences as prologue to develop a more functional set of materials.

This book is about how to do responsible, results-based, people-oriented educational planning. It navigates away from the siren call of identifying and delivering quick-fixes or do-it-now crisis reactions. Instead, there are the proactive concepts and tools required for assisting and encouraging learners to become self-sufficient, self-reliant, contributing members for both today and tomorrow. In our planning we will be able to include individual differences in capabilities and values and have the opportunity to improve our interpersonal relationships and shared destinies.

This book differs from *Educational System Planning* through the addition of new system methods and analytical techniques. At the same time, the successful features of the earlier edition have been retained in an updated and expanded form.

First, what has been added:

- a frame of reference (more accurately, a heuristic) for the planning of educational systems: the Organizational Elements Model (OEM). This "template" allows us to place into perspective all of the resources, methods, and results of education. The OEM allows us to identify and know when we are merely attempting to improve the efficiency of our current efforts (what is) or to precisely identify new objectives and purposes (what should be).
- a nine-step process for assessing educational needs, along with ways and means necessary to collect and use both attitude and perception ("soft") data as well as performance ("hard") data
- distinctions among various types of planning, including strategic, long-range, tactical, and operational, and how and where each is useful
- differentiating among needs assessment, needs analysis, front-end analysis, and other "popular" methods, and showing when to use each
- treatment of a system approach to planning as a two-part approach consisting of identification and verification of needs as the first, and meeting needs as the second
- lessons-learned from the "excellent organizations" literature and the "Japanese Management" approach . . . as well as what we must add to these to make our educational system responsive to our reality, not simply cloning others'
- more on evaluation and system revision and renewal including formative, summative, and goal-free evaluation
- extensive examples and cases-in-point of contemporary educational problems and situations, including an extensive "worked example" from a hypothetical school system

What has been retained, updated, and extended is:

- an emphasis upon a humanistic concern for people, including teachers, learners, administrators, parents, and community members

- a results-orientation with special emphasis added on societal impact and consequences and the "chain of results" which links all learner and teacher accomplishments with school accomplishments and community and societal payoffs
- the steps and tools of educational system analysis, including mission, function, and methods-means analysis
- viewing education in terms of management for results
- a large set of examples from the world of operational education

While it is tempting to believe that we in education are different from other organizations (such as business, military, industry, and government), in fact we have more in common with each other than first meets the eye. The common underlying fabric of any organization is the people in that organization and the clients they serve. Without both, any organization will be out of business. So results-oriented, people-centered planning also serves as survival insurance.

The material in this book has been successfully applied both in educational as well as in other kinds of organizations. If you are not in education, as you use the book, simply replace "education" with "organization."

ROGER KAUFMAN
Tallahassee, Florida

ACKNOWLEDGEMENT

I WISH TO thank many people for their contributions to this book. Certainly my appreciation goes to those who helped *Educational System Planning* come into being. That is *a* basis for what is before you now. Since then, others have made direct and indirect contributions to me. The Florida State University, in general, and Bob Morgan, in particular, provided the atmosphere necessary to prepare this work. My associates, past and present, at the Center for Needs Assessment and Planning have given their advice, counsel, and guidance as we have applied these models and concepts: Bob Stakenas, Michael Knight, Hanna Mayer, Alicia Rojas, Phil Grise, Gabreyesus Hamda, Michael Kane, and others.

Detailed reviews and critiques (often with "bad news" which I didn't want to hear but had to) of this work as it was created, reviewed, edited, changed, and anguished over came from Karen Shader, Jim Klein, Anne Reese, and Cheryl Chase-Kane. These devil's advocates have made this book and its contents much more than it would have been without their specific feedback. Werner Lockley did the final manuscript formatting and readied it for submission.

Long discussions (some casual observers might have called them arguments) with fellw faculty members and graduate students in the Department of Educational Research and the programs in educational psychology, instructional systems, and policy planning at The Florida State University have made my thinking increasingly responsive but far from perfect. Faculty and students at other universities have used some of my evolving concepts and model and have let me know what has been useful and what had to be revised.

Professionals in numerous public and private sector organizations with which I have worked have applied the material and thereby helped to refine the book's contents.

International applications ranging from Australia to The Netherlands, from Canada to Mexico, from Venezuela to Chile have served to educate me about and make me concerned with intercultural, international aspects of educational planning and change. Clifton Chadwick has been of significant assistance in this arena.

As my thinking has evolved, some of it has been published elsewhere. My thanks to the editors of *Educational Technology* and *Performance & Instruction Journal*, both of which have been generous in allowing me to build upon some of that work in this book.

No single volume can supply everything which might be useful to a wide range of readers. Several books will provide additional information on this and related topics:

Kaufman, R. (1982). *Identifying and Solving Problems: A System Approach* (3rd ed.). San Diego:University Associates Publishers.

Kaufman, R. and Stone, B. (1983). *Planning for Organizational Success: A Practical Guide.* New York:John Wiley & Sons, Publishers.

Kaufman, R. and English, F. W. (1979). *Needs Assessment: Concept and Application.* Englewood Cliffs, NJ:Educational Technology Publishers.

My thanks, as well, to these publishers for allowing me to adapt some materials used in these books for this work.

All of the work, effort, and agony which goes into writing a book on educational planning becomes worthwhile when competent and caring professionals read the material, decide what is useful, and attempt to make our educational enterprise increasingly responsive to learners, citizens, educators, and parents of our current and future worlds.

To all of those who have helped me and to those who have dedicated themselves to the measurable and purposive improvement of education and its consequences, my continuing and future thanks and gratitude.

CHAPTER 1

planning—an introduction

THIS IS A book for educators who care—care about results, about learner individuality and performance, about helping learners create a better future for themselves and society. The "system approach"[1] process for educational system planning provided in this book is about how to build and manage a successful educational system. The approach details a way of thinking that can help dedicated professionals to create results that they have long sought. It is designed to help achieve human success and dignity where they do not exist, and to increase them where they only partially exist.

This holistic system approach has a number of distinguishing characteristics:

(a) It is results oriented.

(b) It places each individual learner at the center of educational planning and management.

(c) It is a precise way of assuring that the social and personal uniqueness of each person is formally brought to the forefront of planning.

(d) It emphasizes that both a learner's current and future success are important.

useful, humane results

An Educational System Planning Approach Should Help Make Education Humane

Educational success presupposes that the individuality of each person is considered and preserved in the design and application of

---

[1]For those impatient for a definition, one may be found in the glossary at the end of this chapter.

any educational process. Planning and the tools of a system approach focus on the learner and assure that each one's ambitions, capabilities, future potential, hopes, and aspirations are considered and developed. This is important enough to be done precisely, accurately, and systematically.

Precision and planning are really humanizing. Maintaining rigor and caring about accomplishing useful results can be our best assurance that learners are not forced into arbitrary molds and categories, either by ignorance or by lack of appropriate tools for making education individually responsive. In his book *Future Shock*, Alvin Toffler (1970) makes the point well:

> "Arguing that planning imposes values on the future, the anti-planners overlook the fact that non-planning does so, too—often with far worse consequences."

Not to plan at all, or not to plan on the basis of defining individual needs, wants, realities, and characteristics, is to risk the degradation of the learner's uniqueness, happiness, dignity, potential, and ability. A system approach (what this book is about) is a responsive process for reasonably and responsibly identifying educational goals and objectives and resolving educational problems. It is useful, but it can be only as good as the people using it allow and demand.

Planning is simply a substitute for good luck (Schuck, cited in Kaufman, 1972). If things are satisfactory the way they are now, you don't have to go to the trouble of planning. If things could and should be better, then positive, planned change using the approach presented here will provide a tool for assuring that change is humanely planned and useful.

change

As educators, we can deal with change in several ways. We can be spectators to change, or we may be participants in it. All too often we are bystanders and are swept along with conditions which cause us to constantly <u>react</u> to situational crises. We may even delay decisions until others make them for us.

Today, most educational agencies are involved in change. Students, teachers, parents, and special interest groups are becoming better organized in their demands for change and often are quite expert in exerting pressure for and against specific educational programs and procedures. Changes are demanded of educators, frequently as if a single special topic or approach were the only critical element of an entire educational program.

Educational laws are growing bulkier and more intricate. Legislators are passing laws concerning educational practices, accountability, and procedures at a rate that requires most educators to be speed readers, oracles, and magicians. "Excellence" is often mandated but not defined, and demands keep growing. Wherever we are in education, there are pressures for us to be elsewhere.

If we simply react to demands for change, a type of anarchy may result, in which we try to be everywhere at the same time and probably satisfy none of our clients (i.e., those whom we are attempting to serve).

Action, on the other hand, requires purpose, confidence, and important results. When we act rather than react, we become accountable for both the educational processes and their payoffs. The responsibility is ours; we make a professional commitment to be proactive.

An action-oriented system approach to education requires that systematic and formal planning, design, implementation, evaluation, and responsive revisions take place. There is a constant effort to achieve relevancy and practicality for the learners, so that they may survive, be self-sufficient, form satisfying relationships with others, and contribute in and to society when they leave our educational agencies (Kaufman, 1972; 1982). Open, observable, and accountable, a system approach strives to identify priority needs and requirements and moves to meet them efficiently and effectively. This approach allows for temporary failure in that when we fall short of our objectives, the results signal the requirement for revision.

The cliché that change is inevitable is still appropriate. The question for educators seems to be whether we will be the masters or the victims of change. Change, however, seems to be threatening to virtually everyone. Beals (1968) states: " . . . the technological innovation which sooner or later arouses no resistance must be extremely trivial." When an educator decides to change (or innovate), she must be prepared to meet resistance from many sources—teachers, parents, administrators, the school board, and other members of the community.

The threat from change is unfortunately a necessary price of relevancy. To remain static is to await decay and evolutionary extinction; to react is to risk dissipation of energy without achieving relevancy; to innovate and act to increase our responsiveness to other people is to invite criticism. Practical, functional, justifiable, planned change is a professional responsibility, and it is suggested that a system approach will help define and plan useful and functional change.

Education is both subject to and sensitive to change. New educational methods and techniques are always being introduced and tried, although not always on the most sensible bases. In fact, educators often are accused of pursuing new methods with nothing but hope and faith to guide them. Any useful planning approach must avoid change for its own sake. There is nothing as frightening as ignorance in action. Therefore, action has the greatest chance for success when valid data are used to identify practical and realistic purposes. Not to initiate innovative and responsible change is riskier than standing still (Drucker, 1985); otherwise the world and reality will overtake you.

A system approach which is rational and logical rather than simply quick-fix-oriented or based on historical precedent may be difficult to "sell" to people who operate only on an intuitive or "self-protection" basis. Yet meaningful progress has been made by the individual who, armed only with a valid requirement and a useful process, has set out and achieved an appropriate change. "Find a need and fill it" has been good advice that has been given to young people for some time. The approach to planning which follows provides a process for finding the needs and the best way of meeting them.

Happily, there is a trend in education away from the sole use of raw intuition, historical precedence, and conventional wisdom, and toward formal methods for information gathering and use. It is increasingly acceptable and expected for any agency to collect and apply precision and reality in any planning and subsequent activity. This shift is not in curriculum content alone but also in the design and management of the entire educational system.

The purposive inclusion of the values of all educational partners (learners, educators, parents, and community) in the planning process is essential. Without the human concern for and about people, any changes will be difficult if not impossible. Toffler (1980) noted in *The Third Wave* that "high tech" must be accompanied with "high touch" (the concern for human feelings and worth), if technological innovation is to succeed. Through modern history, he noted, any time the human element in change has been ignored (or assumed), failure emerged. This planning approach (which is in itself a technology of planning) formally includes "high touch" in its nature and use.

some beginnings of educational system planning

System(s) approaches have been with us for some time. They have helped us to understand educational purposes and organization as well as account for the interactions among the system parts when planning, designing, developing, managing, evaluating, and changing.

System concepts came into vogue among human performance specialists during the 1960s and 1970s. Many alternative models were offered under a variety of names including educational engineering, systems approach, system approach, and systematic approach, including those of Branson, et al., 1976; Buckley, 1968; Carter, 1969; Churchman, 1969; Cleland and King, 1968 and 1969; Corrigan, 1975; Gagne, 1962; Gilbert, 1971; Kaufman, 1968 and 1972; Meals, 1967; Morgan and Chadwick, 1971; and Silvern, 1968. All models had several features in common:

- results-orientation
- clear, measurable objectives
- systematic procedures for reaching stated objectives
- accounting for the dynamic relationship among the parts of the system
- requirement for continuous evaluation and revision

Some Limitations of Older Models

These models targeted the improvement of human performance subsystems (including educational concerns), stimulated thought, generated articles, and gave impetus, aid, and encouragement to many methodological contributions dealing with fragments of a total system approach which both identifies needs and then finds the best ways and means to meet them. These splinters included (but were not limited to) measurable objectives, media selection and delivery, task analysis, program evaluation review techniques (PERT), management by objectives, learning hierarchies, methods-means selection, formative evaluation, summative evaluation, goal-free evaluation, instructional design and development, front-end analysis, problem analysis, educational television, multi-media, programmed instruction, needs assessment, needs analysis, computer-assisted learning, and system planning. Sometimes (and inaccurately) these techniques are referred to under the label "systems approaches."

The linking of such methods as the ones listed above with system(s) models was exhilarating but usually frustrating, since our intentions always seemed to exceed our results. The models and approaches gave, however, focus to the fact that we could (if we wanted) predictably improve individual learner mastery.

These older systems approaches tended to concentrate on fragmented parts of a larger system rather than taking on the more holistic problems and context (such as people and organizations operating in a societal environment) of the larger system itself. By so doing, the users focused, one-at-a-time, on the small and more controllable educational variables (such as teaching behavior, measurable objectives, instructional improvement, subject-matter content), and traded possible greater impact for fleeting simplicity. These older efforts and models have tended to accentuate the known and simple, and ignore or deprecate the complex and holistic.

Simpler is not always better. Many educational practitioners often seek simplicity. It may be valued because it seems easier to communicate (sell) decision-makers with linear, uncomplicated concepts. Good intentions don't necessarily yield useful results. We can be more realistic. If we are to be successful educational system planners and improvers, we should include the total educational context, not just one or two slivers of it.

These older models differ in their assumed (or stated) starting place for educational planning. Systems models focused primarily on organizational or learning objectives. The system (no third "s") models, evolving at the same time with the other models, encouraged defining goals and objectives external to the organization as the proper starting place for educational planning (Kaufman, Corrigan & Johnson, 1969; Kaufman, 1972; Kaufman, 1982). Systematic approaches simply require things to be trackable and repeatable, and thus can be a part of a system or systems approach. Still, confusion among these models and approaches reigns, for the words are similar, and only the devoted understand that there might be some real differences underneath the overt semantic squabbling. People, their shared destinies and well-being, are much too important to assume or ignore. Only a system approach formally considers the individual and collective good of and for people.

Another characteristic of older approaches is that they tended to be reactive rather than allowing the user to create a better future. In using an analytic-deductive approach, the user often assumed the validity and utility of existing goals and objectives rather than perceived an opportunity to plan and identify gaps between current system consequences and those which could be sought, and inductively to identify and achieve useful alternative futures. While the "systems" approaches were gaining attention and use, more holistic concerns were also being considered and developed. The approach presented here is both inductive (identifying and seeking to achieve a better future) and analytic-deductive (effectively and efficiently improving the current system in order to achieve existing goals and objectives). Older approaches tend to make the current system more efficient in reaching current goals and objectives, while this one also helps to identify new visions and identify new outcomes.

Often ignored in existing models of planning is the fact that educational systems are means to societal ends. Individuals working in educational agencies are likewise means to educational ends. Students who go through our schools are being prepared to be successful and contribute in society. Learning does not stop at the schoolhouse door, and educational experiences should encourage persons to be inquiring throughout life. Following are some of the basic concepts involved in defining and planning realistic, learner-oriented educational systems which will be responsive to today's and tomorrow's worlds.

a holistic focus

Recently, educational planning concern has swung from an atomistic or singular preoccupation with instructional design and teaching improvement alone to more global, holistic concerns. These "big-picture" applications not only use and apply performance analysis to individual activities, but also add the requirement for a system-wide identification and analysis of opportunities and problems. Because of this concern for subject matter and also for the usefulness of what learners know and do in later life, macro techniques and interventions have been applied in education, including system analysis, policy analysis, system planning, strategic planning, long-range planning, human resource development, quality circles, and management development. Educators are now looking at the whole as well as each of the parts of their educational systems.

Perhaps this interest in more holistic concerns came in part from the successes (both real and imagined) of instructional design and development—if we can improve individual learner and teacher performance, why not attempt to take on the entire educational establishment? The concern for individual performance and the concern for educational performance differ only in degree, not in kind.

While it is more tangible to work with learning problems associated with a specific subject-matter (e.g., reading, special education, bookkeeping, vocational education, social studies, computers), the targeting of an entire school system as a performance improvement client greatly increases the complexity of analysis while offering exhilarating payoff possibilities for defining and delivering excellence.

"Excellence," "Japanese Management," and System Planning

The educational literature has increasingly noticed the concern in business for "excellence" and "Japanese management." There are some useful lessons here. (However, it would probably be a mistake to blindly copy these approaches.) Successful Western and Eastern organizations and those who would be "excellent" both seem to have common characteristics (cf. Pascale & Athos, 1981; Peters & Waterman, 1982; Peters & Austin, 1985; Peters, 1987; Kanter, 1983; Kaufman, 1984). Those include:

- concern for the client's success and well-being
- responsiveness to client's needs
- not making excuses for failures but learning from them
- cooperative relationships with clients
- almost fanatic attention to detail and quality
- listening and learning
- concern for the society and community around the organization

An interesting common focus of "excellent" organizations is a deep and genuine concern for the client, not just making a profit (if you are a business) or delivering a service. A caring and abiding focus on improving the client's success in the client's world is a "hallmark" of successful business organizations as well as educational ones (Kaufman, 1984; Kaufman & Stone, 1983; Peters & Waterman, 1982; Peters & Austin, 1985; Peters, 1987). Successful organizations obtain their goals and rewards from the external world, not from just within their own agencies. This type of excellence is exactly what a system approach attempts to deliver.

The material in this book provides an integrated and holistic definition for a system approach. This model recommends starting the planning process with external (e.g., what it takes to "make it" in the world) as well as internal (e.g., mastering subjects) needs assessments. It moves systematically from "what is" to "what should be"—a two-phase system model. This model, therefore, encompasses other models: systems and systematic approaches. It promises to be more useful than other approaches by virtue of its external, outside-the-school societal starting place, while also maintaining the discipline and rigor of previous models. It also identifies new visions and purposes, not simply finding ways and means to achieve status quo objectives.

The Importance of Including Societal Impact as a Focus of Educational System Planning

Education, in line with other "excellent" organizations, should help learners be successful in school and in later life. In addition, each learner should be able to contribute to society in order to make the world a better and more satisfying place to live and work, both for herself and others. If we are going to provide learning opportunities to be used by students both in and outside school, we should plan that way. Educational goals and objectives, therefore, should be based upon that which is required to survive and be self-sufficient and self-reliant in the current and future world. The planning process should include the social sensitivities and skills to forge cooperative relationships with others. Learners as well as our schools should be continually growing and improving in response to a changing world and changing realities.

To simply base educational planning on courses and mastery of content is to assume that the learning of material will automatically make the learner successful in later life. Such an assumption is risky. Much of educational planning and delivery now is concerned only with pieces, or splinters, of education, such as those in Figure 1.1.

Mastery or completion of any one of the splinters is not enough for a student to be certified as competent, or for a school system to believe that it has been successful. Passing individual courses does not make one educated.

To function in life, any graduate or completer should be able to draw upon that which was learned in school by selecting from the various "splinters" of the curriculum those which will be useful and by applying them correctly when they are required. The integration of that which has been learned, the selection and proper "bundling" of the appropriate pieces of that which has been acquired, is a "secret of success" for those who are either very clever or very lucky . . . or who, formally or informally, apply a holistic approach.

Rather than depending upon luck or cleverness, system planning should relate the splinters of curriculum and schooling to current and changing life requirements. We could conceive of this integration by viewing the "splinters of education" (such as those in Figure 1.1) as part of larger and larger units (represented in Figure 1.2). In

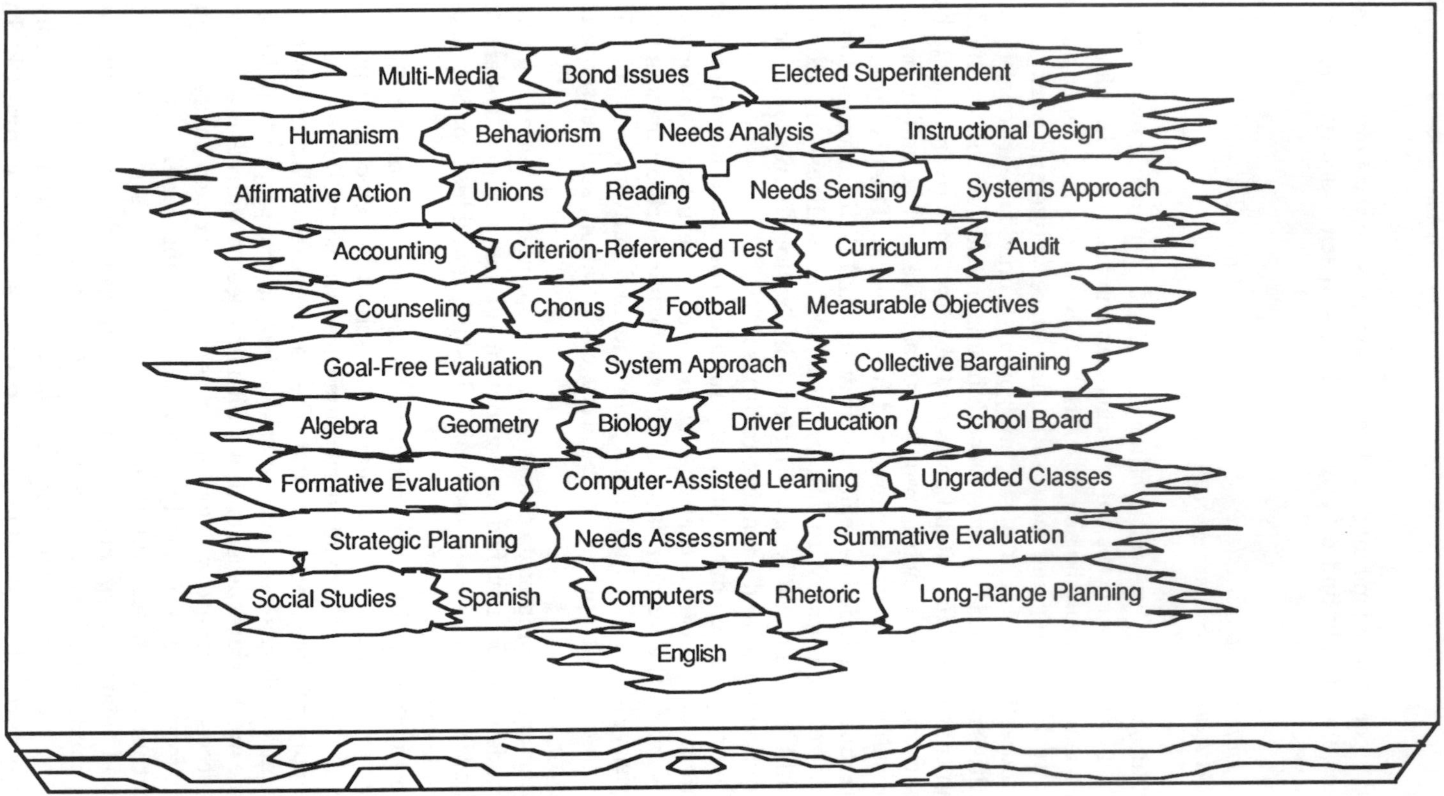

Figure 1.1. Some of the components, or "splinters," of education.

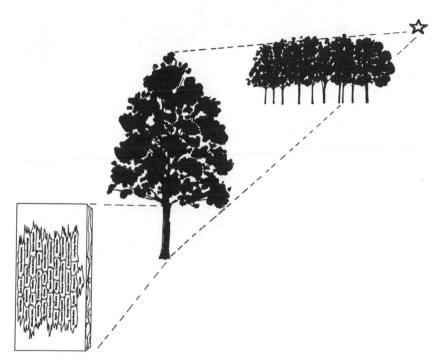

Figure 1.2. Integrating the "splinters" of educational activities, content, and curriculum in order to make a positive societal impact. Based, in part, upon Kaufman, 1983a. Reprinted by permission of the *Performance & Instruction Journal,* © 1983.

this analogy, the splinters form a board. Perhaps this board could represent a course of study, or an educational program. This board, made up of splinters, could be then seen as a part of a larger unit (symbolized as a tree) which might represent the curriculum of an elementary or high school. The "tree," in turn, may be seen as a part of a larger unit (symbolically a forest) such as the entire educational experience. Finally, carrying this further, there is an outside-of-the-system referent (shown as an external navigational point, or a "North Star") to emphasize that all of the things that go on in schools are still part of, and subsystems of, the external world. This external "North Star" is positive societal impact . . . that which schools are supposed to teach learners how to achieve and contribute, and a set of results towards which all may steer.

The design, development, implementation, evaluation, and revision of any educational system should include the external, outside-of-education realities, which is a viable alternative to depending upon good luck.

Let's start identifying some parts of an educational system planning process (using a system approach) which is humanistic, practical, future-oriented, and results-based. Material in subsequent chapters will build on these.

some definitions and basic concepts

One of the most difficult aspects of dealing with a new or unfamiliar discipline—educational system planning, for example—is terminology. Frequently, unfamiliar words are dismissed as "jargon," with the result that communication really cannot take place. Each time a word or concept appears in this book, it will be precisely defined, often with a practical example. Clarity and rigor are important, since different educators use the same words but without common meanings, and thus communication breaks down. In order to help avoid this, some definitions are given below.

SYSTEM

The sum total of parts working independently and working together to achieve specified required results, or outcomes,[2] based on needs. For example, a school, a school district, or a university could all be systems (if each had purpose), and an instructional program could also be a system. According to this definition, if an entity has defined purpose and organization, it can be a system.

ENDS

The results, impacts, or accomplishments achieved. There are three types of results: (1) learner or teacher accomplishments, which are building blocks for major results (such as completing a course, or passing a test); (2) school accomplishments which transcend the educational organization (such as a graduates or completers); and (3) the societal results and payoffs of educational results (e.g., keeping a job, voting, having financial credit, supporting oneself).

---

[2] "Outcome" is one of several words which have a specific meaning when used in this book. Such words with specific meanings will be defined in the glossary at the end of the chapter, and will be discussed in detail in Chapter 2. For now, "outcome" is the societal consequences of that which an educational organization uses, does, produces, and delivers.

End ◄─ Possible Means ─► End
End ◄─ Possible Means ─► End
End ◄─ Possible Means ─► End
End ◄─ Possible Means ─► End

Figure 1.3. A need (when using a system approach) is a gap between two results, or ends. Means are the possible ways of closing those gaps.

OBJECTIVE

A statement of an end, or result, to be accomplished (cf. Mager, 1975). A measurable objective includes precise, clear, and mutually understood statements of:

- what results are to be accomplished
- who or what will display that which has been accomplished
- under what conditions the results will be observed
- what criteria will be used to determine accomplishment (or non-accomplishment)

MEANS

Any process, resource, method or technique which delivers a result (or end). (Most English words ending with the suffix "ing" as a means: educating, teaching, learning, planning, testing, managing. . . .)

NEED

A measurable discrepancy, or gap, between current and desired results. The word "need" has several possible (and indeed popular) meanings (Komisar, 1961). The one used here is that which identifies and documents a gap in results, not a gap in resources or processes (Figure 1.3). The term "quasi-need" is used to describe a gap in processes, how-to-do-its, inputs, or resources.

"Need." We use that word a lot. Maybe too much. The dictionary gives us lots of room with it, allowing its use as both a noun and a verb. Dictionaries are nice that way: they provide both definitions and common usage. Flexibility. Elbow room. The use of "need" as a verb sounds imperative: "I need to go to town," "I need to train supervisors," "We need more money." In fact, when it is used as a verb, it dictates to us what solutions (e.g., training, more money) to use regardless of the presenting problem. As a noun, it specifies the gaps in results (90% of those trained are successful on the job while those not trained run a rate of 33%; profits are down 300%

(continued)

from last year). It makes us ask ourselves "if training is the solution, what is the problem?" Means and ends. "Need" as a verb speaks to means, "need" as a noun speaks to gaps in results.

"Motive." We don't use that word so much anymore, but we use the concept. We have seminars to motivate others, and we want our children, friends, and co-workers to be "motivated" (ideally towards a worthy end defined as a result). We most often use the word to refer to the amount of energy, drive, push, grit, or resources we will commit to getting from "what is" to "what should be." Motivation is a measure of how hard we will work or how much we will commit to achieve some result, what we will devote, give up, or use to reach a goal.

In popular usage, we tend to mix up these two words and their meanings. When we use "need" as a verb (or in a verb sense, such as "I have a need to eat") we most likely are talking about motivation. In fact, Maslow's famed (and fabled) "hierarchy of needs" is really a hierarchy of motivators: it shows how much we will ante up to close a gap in results, with the most impelling being physiological, then safety, right up his scale through self-actualization. If we don't have a gap in results, there is really a very small role for motivation. No need (no gap in results), no problem, no motivation to meet the need.

So what? What's the big deal? When sitting around chewing the fat, or rapping with a client, we always know what we mean, even if we do use "need" as a verb, use it instead of "motive." What's in a word anyway? Plenty. We know that words are important symbols: they "stand for" real events or things. Most of us would not think of using "he" as a generic for males and females for a good reason: there are two sexes, and constantly referring to women as "he" causes role confusion and female role diminishment.

Words are important, and the more precisely we use them, the less likely we are to confuse that which they symbolize. If we mean a gap in results, let's be precise about that, and if we mean motive, let's say that. It turns out that in the operational world of human performance improvement the implications for confusing "need" and "motive" are manifest.

Most performance improvement specialists are "doers." We like to get results, demonstrate them and take pride in getting from "what is" to "what should be." We like to get results so much that we often move into action before we know the problem, before we have defined and justified the exact gaps in results to be closed. We often justify jumping into a solution (training, for example) by saying "we need training," before defining the gaps in performance and the fact that training will be the best way to close those gaps. We even have people running around asking for "training needs assessments" as if we already know that training is the right solution to the existing problems. But "we *need* training" has a ring of urgency to it! We have justified our desire to do training by speaking to our motivation to do it. We did not first identify, define, and justify our gaps in results—needs—before launching into our training solution. We confuse means (our motives, our training solution) with ends (our documented performance gaps).[3]

[3]Reprinted by permission, © *Performance & Instruction*, 1986.

For system planning it is important not to include in the statement of need any solution, or how-to-do-it, for getting from current results to desired ones. Including a solution in a statement of need automatically reduces the options for meeting a need, and thus cuts down on the probability of finding new, innovative, or creative ways of bridging the gap. To repeat: when one includes a solution in a statement of need, there is a risk of jumping from unwarranted assumptions to foregone conclusions; choosing a solution before the problem has been identified and selected might leave us unresponsive to the real concerns and gaps which exist in our educational world.

NEEDS ASSESSMENT

The process of identifying, scoping, documenting, and justifying needs, placing them in priority order, and selecting those for reduction or elimination. Needs assessments will identify both internal (educational) and external (societal) gaps in results. These needs will provide the data base for later identifying that which is working well, what is not, what to keep, and what to change. It is the topic of Chapter 3.

NEEDS ANALYSIS

After a need is identified, it may then be analyzed into its constituent component parts, determining what each part does and how each contributes to the whole. Needs analyses, in practice, tend to focus on methods and means and their failure to deliver useful results. Thus, most needs analyses tend to be solutions-oriented. System analysis (see below and Chapters 4, 5, and 6) is useful for doing a needs analysis.

PROBLEM

A need selected for resolution. (No gap in results, no need; no need, no problem.)

SYSTEM APPROACH

A process by which needs are identified and documented, problems are selected, requirements for problem solution are identified, solutions are chosen from alternatives, methods and means are obtained and implemented, results are evaluated, and required revisions to all or part of the system are made so that the needs are reduced or eliminated.

A system approach, as used here, is a rational and logical problem-solving process for identifying and resolving important educational problems. It is central to educational system planning (which is perhaps better termed educational success planning).

A system approach (Kaufman, 1987a) has two distinct parts or phases:

- identifying, scoping, selecting and prioritizing needs (needs assessment)
- eliminating or reducing the needs (problem solving)

Thus defined, a system approach is both a process tool for more effectively and efficiently defining and achieving required educational outcomes and a mode of thinking that emphasizes problem identification and problem resolution. It utilizes a formulation of rational, logical problem-solving techniques that has become increasingly familiar and useful in management, physical and behavioral sciences, and human communication.

SYSTEM ANALYSIS

Identifies the requirements and functions in order for a system to meet its goals and objectives. There are several tools for system analysis: mission analysis, function analysis, and methods-means analysis. Unlike needs analysis, system analysis may be proactive and identifies that which should be accomplished, while needs analysis finds the causes for current system operation. System analysis (a prime tool for doing a needs analysis) most relates to the system approach phase of planning that which is required in order to "get from what is to what should be."

As science and scientific methodology are processes, so are planning and a system approach processes. The usefulness of this process depends on:

(1) The validity of the data that are used to identify and resolve educational problems

(2) The objectivity of the people using a system approach and its associated tools in planning

PLAN

A determination of what needs and associated objectives are to be met and what functions must be completed to meet the needs.

STRATEGIC, TACTICAL, LONG-RANGE, AND OPERATIONAL PLANNING

Strategic planning asks and answers the question "Where is society going, where should it be going, and how can our educational agency make a positive contribution?" Tactical planning involves the acceptance of existing educational goals and seeks to apply the most effective and efficient ways and means of getting them accomplished. Long-range planning takes existing educational objectives which have long lead-times (they will have to be met in 3–5 years, for instance) and helps make certain that they will be accomplished. Operational planning identifies what has to be done now . . . on a current day-to-day basis.

All of these domains of planning are important for the success of any educational agency. They are not the same, however.

All of the varieties of planning may utilize or build from a system approach.

ORGANIZATIONAL EFFORTS

The laws, policies, regulations, needs, wants, values, resources, and personnel which an educational agency may or must use. These are the "ingredients" of educational planning and doing. Given these "ingredients," organizational efforts apply the methods, techniques, and activities in order to deliver educational results.

ORGANIZATIONAL RESULTS

Those educational products and outputs that the organizational efforts deliver. There are two types of educational organizational results. One includes the "building blocks" of teacher and learner accomplishments (such as a passed test, a completed course, a mastered musical instrument, a completed intramural football game). The second type of result combines all those of the first type into a composite which the educational agency delivers outside of itself (e.g., a high school graduate, a certificate awarded in automotive mechanics, having obtained a job for which trained).

SOCIETAL CONSEQUENCES

Those consequences that the organizational results (e.g., the graduates) have in and for society. Indicators of positive societal payoffs include citizens who vote, earning more than one spends, being enrolled in higher education, being gainfully employed, and enjoying a positive quality of life. In this book, these societal results are also called "outcomes."

Organizational efforts, organizational results, and societal consequences describe any educational enterprise:

Organizational Efforts ---▶ Organizational Results ---▶ Societal Consequences

A practical needs assessment is a process for determining the gaps between What Is and What Should Be for <u>results</u> (although some approaches inappropriately only look at gaps in resources and procedures—best termed Quasi-Needs Assessment—(Kaufman, Stakenas, Wager, & Mayer, 1981). It allows an educational planner to relate organizational efforts, organizational results, and societal impact.

How are these concepts and tools used? When should they be used? What will each of them do? They are important parts of educational system planning, and will be called upon as we identify and define educational requirements and solve educational problems. So let's take a look at the basic steps in educational system planning.

education, planning, and management

Education occurs in a context of values—what do the various partners of education require and expect? The public provides funds and resources for educators to achieve that which they value. Regardless of whether the requirements are well defined, the public still holds educators responsible for outcomes and for utilization of resources. Education has its expression through a series of products, outputs, and outcomes (results) which the process is expected to achieve. The educational system cannot afford to be simply reactive to popular cries for what and how it teaches, but should help set the agenda for the future: a more productive, humane, and useful future.

The educational process may be managed, mismanaged, or fall in between these extremes. An overall educational system approach management process model (Kaufman, 1987a) consists of the following two elements:

- identify, scope, and select needs
- get from "what is" to "what should be"

The management tool useful for identifying, scoping, and selecting needs is "needs assessment."

The management tool for getting from "what is" to "what should be" is a six-step process called "problem solving":

(1) Identify (or verify) problem (based upon documented needs).

(2) Determine solution requirements and alternative solutions.

(3) Select solutions (from among the alternatives).

(4) Implement selected solutions (to achieve the required results).

(5) Determine performance effectiveness and efficiency.

(6) Revise as required at any step in the process.

Any time educational change is to occur, this six-step process may be used. It is a closed-loop or self-correcting process; at each step there is a requirement to determine whether the plan is succeeding and decide whether to revise or continue. In planning we may identify all elements and requirements for achieving valid change utilizing the suggested six-step management process.

The major focus of this book is on problem identification, verification, and scoping, plus the tools, procedures, and logic of needs assessment and problem solving (actually problem-resolving). It is a forward-looking approach which is not content only to do more efficiently that which we are currently doing. The "doing" aspects of a complete system approach (termed "system synthesis") are briefly described and related to planning. The emphasis here, then, is determining what to do, and mastering the tools of responsible planning. Armed with these skills, and with the aid of a number of good references in this area, the reader may plan the necessary "doing" (or synthesis) aspects of a system approach.

Educational System Planning Is Practical

As Sechrest (personal communication) has noted "mediocrity is so easy to achieve, there is no point in planning for it." If one is satisfied with the status quo, or if whatever happens will be satisfactory, there is no requirement to do planning, use a system approach, identify needs, or resolve problems. But most of us want to achieve increasingly useful results—on purpose. A system approach is a proactive way by which a planner may identify needs and eliminate them.

Planning best starts with the identification of needs—the measurable discrepancy (or gap) between current outcomes and desired or required ones. There are, perhaps, several ways of stating this gap, such as "the measurable discrepancy between 'what is' and 'what is required.'" The important concept is that to have a need we must identify and document that there is a gap between two results, that which is currently occurring and that which should occur. The setting of the two polar dimensions of a need should be done in a formal way, called "needs assessment."

A needs assessment provides data for identifying high-priority needs for subsequent elimination. Needs, when documented, provide the basic information for setting valid goals to better assure us that our educational products and outputs are relevant.

By identifying required outcomes (or results) first, and then deciding about the most effective and efficient "process," we forestall the likelihood of employing solutions that do not meet the actual needs. Since planning provides a method for identifying such needs and goals, it allows us to decide on a "map" of action (or accomplishment blueprint) to guide our efforts and our money toward relevant success.

It is not unusual to hear citizens and educators alike protest "we already know what our problems are, what we 'need' are solutions." This frequently is not an accurate perception. Usually, they sense some symptoms of a problem without knowing the exact nature of the problem.

If we attempt to solve poorly defined problems, we are faced with (1) an infinite number of possible solutions, and/or (2) a situation in which we treat only the symptoms and never really get at the basic problems. The analogy would be a physician who prescribed aspirin for a headache only to later find out that the patient had a brain tumor. It is critical not to confuse means and ends, and not to efface or ignore the important distinction between results and processes (ways of achieving results)!

The commitment to planning before swinging into action can prevent educators from selecting how we are going to do something before we know what should be done. It also will keep us from merely treating symptoms (with marginal success or perhaps even failure).

Planning is first and foremost concerned with determining <u>what</u> is to be accomplished so that practical how-to-do-it decisions may be made later. Planning comes before doing. Planning is a process for determining "where to go" and identifying the requirements for getting there in the most effective and efficient manner possible.

Managing Education: Asking and Answering Important Questions

Planning will help pose important questions and find the most effective and efficient answers. Some of the more important management questions and the tools which may be used to answer them are provided in Table 1.1.

TABLE 1.1 Educational management questions and responsive tools to answer each.

Management Questions	System Planning Tools
What are our current results and payoffs, and what results and payoffs should we seek?	Needs Assessment
What intermediate results are required to get from where we are to where we want to be (and what are the possible ways of getting these results)?	System Analysis
What major functions have to be completed to get from here to there?	Mission Analysis
What are the specific origins, sources and causes of the existing needs and problems?	Needs Analysis
What are the educational needs and what must be accomplished to meet them effectively and efficiently?	Educational System Planning
What type of planning best assures that all of the pieces (or subsystems) work together to identify and achieve success?	System Approach

summary

A system approach to education is a problem identification and resolution process. It is useful to educators who want relevant and predictable learner-oriented results. The relation between the results we want to accomplish (ends) and the best ways of delivering them (means) may be placed into perspective by a planning approach which is the subject of this book. The "hallmark" of this approach includes concepts and tools along with a rationale calling for the identification of human and organizational needs and their associated problems, before solutions are identified and selected. Another feature of this approach is its inclusion of positive societal impact in educational planning. It looks to identify and deliver a better tomorrow, not just make today's efforts and approaches more efficient.

The self-correcting nature of a system approach better assures an objective basis for learning and educational management. Educators are becoming more logical and analytical, and a system approach is a useful way of getting important results.

The process described in this book will provide the educator who intends to make useful, systematic, organized change with the necessary information for achieving new educational success. Additionally it will supply a realistic rationale for any such change. This process does not automatically assume that everything going on now is bad, nor does it assume that everything is useful or that every proposed change is potentially good! It intends to keep the worthwhile and useful, and also to help identify areas in which new and more successful ways and means can guide us in order to assist every learner to be both successful in school as well as in later life.

glossary

Educational system planning   the identification of needs, and the determination of what must be accomplished to effectively and efficiently meet the needs. Tools used include needs assessment and system analysis.

End   a result, impact, or accomplishment.

Means   any input, process, method, technique, or how-to-do-it which leads to a result, or end. These constitute organizational efforts.

Need   the measurable discrepancy between "where we are now" and "where we should be," in terms of outcomes, or results.

Needs analysis   the identification of the causes or origins of needs and possible ways of meeting them.

Needs assessment   the formal process for identifying discrepancies in results, placing them in priority order, and selecting the most critical for closure.

Objective   a statement of intended result which precisely states what result is to be accomplished, who or what will display the result, under what conditions the result will be observed, and what exact criteria will be used to determine completion.

Organizational efforts   The rules, laws, policies, regulations, needs, wants, values, resources, and personnel which an educational agency may or must use. These are the "ingredients," or inputs, of educational planning and doing which are put into use. Also a part of organizational efforts are the activities (e.g., teaching, learning, presenting) of education.

Organizational results   those products (learner and teacher accomplishments) and outputs (school accomplishments) that the organizational efforts deliver.

Outcome   the societal impact or consequences of an output.

Output   the collected products which an educational agency can or does deliver for institutions beyond itself (such as a graduate).

Plan   a projection of what is to be accomplished to reach valid and valued goals.

Problem   a need selected for reduction or elimination.

Process   the ways and means for achieving any result. A means.

Product   the basic en-route educational result which, by itself is not usually useful, but is part of the overall outputs which can or will be delivered outside of the educational agency.

System   the sum total of parts working independently and working together to achieve required results based upon needs.

System approach   a two-part process by which (1) needs are identified, documented, justified, and associated problems are selected, and (2) requirements for problem solution are identified, solutions are selected from alternatives, methods and means are obtained and implemented, results are evaluated, and required revisions to all or part of the system are made so that the needs are eliminated or reduced.

Systematic approach   the doing of functions on an orderly, predictable basis. One may be systematic and wrong, however. A system approach can include the features of both a systems and a systematic approach.

Systems approach   an approach which, while accounting for each part of the system having effects on all other parts, seeks to find the most effective and efficient ways and means to meet the already established objectives.

Societal consequences   those results and impacts that the delivered organizational results have in and for society.

exercises

1. The definition for planning used in this book is:

2. A system approach, as used in this book, is defined as: (Use your own words—remember that these are concepts, not fodder for blind memorization.)

3. A system approach is (choose one): (a) the use of innovative hardware and software in education, (b) a tool for selecting technology, (c) a method based on computer technology, (d) a process for planning and doing.

4. Discuss, either pro or con, the following: "If used properly, a system approach to education can make education more humane."

5. Realistic planning starts with an identification of:

6. What is needs assessment?

7. What is the relation between means and ends?

8. Give the two basic elements of an overall management process as defined here:

    a.
    b.

9. Define an educational need:

10. What are "organizational efforts," "organizational results," and "societal consequences?" How are these useful in any organization (and not just educational ones)?

11. What are the differences between "needs" and "wants?"

12. Define and give a possible application for each of the following:
Strategic planning:
Tactical planning:
Long-range planning:
Operational planning:

13. What are the advantages and disadvantages of a "system approach" as defined here?

14. What are the differences among "system approach," "systematic approach," and "systems approach"?

15. Identify some areas in your educational agency where means and ends might have been confused, and what a system approach might do to rectify the situation.

16. Why should "societal good" be the basis of educational planning and doing?

17. Why is it important to use a planning approach which uses both an analytic-deductive approach as well as an inductive one?

CHAPTER 2

education as a management process

THIS CHAPTER PROVIDES an overview of the basic concepts and tools for planning educational systems. This system approach divides into two major clusters: needs assessment and problem solving. Needs assessment is a discrepancy analysis which helps us to determine where we are now and where we should be going. Problem solving builds from that base, and helps to identify the requirements for whatever action we should take.

The nature of the two major clusters and each of their associated tools and techniques may not become altogether clear until each has been detailed in the chapters which follow. In system fashion (where each part interacts with all others while having the same overall purpose), each part will be identified and described, and then the total approach will be integrated into a system approach to the planning of educational systems.

Education itself may be viewed as a process for providing learners with (at least minimal) skills, knowledge, abilities, and attitudes, so that they may live and produce in our society when they legally exit from our educational agencies. The output of education is no less than the achievement of these required minimal skills, knowledges, abilities, and attitudes. The behavior and achievements of learners as they function as citizens in today's and tomorrow's worlds determine whether the required outcome has been achieved. In addition to the minimal skills, information, attitudes, and abilities to be self-sufficient and self-reliant, we should provide learning opportunities in the areas of self- and societal growth and improvement. Everyone should be able to make a living as well as contribute to the improvement of their selves and world.

It is useful to conceive of the educator—an administrator, a counselor, a teacher, a planner, or a curriculum specialist—as a manager of the learning process. The management of learning opportunities involves the ascertainment of the needs of learners, educators, and society, and then the identification of problems, and the application of appropriate procedures in order to fashion an educational system responsive to these. The product of this management process is identical to the product of education: the required skills, knowledge, abilities, and attitudes of learners.

management, accountability, and results

The educational manager's job is to plan, design, and implement an efficient and effective educational and learning system responsive to the needs of learners, educators, and society. Successful management requires accountability for the outcomes of the system. Outcomes are specified in measurable performance terms, and achievement of them is openly determined and reported in order that appropriate revision and redesign may take place.

Of course, the educational agencies of our nation cannot be completely responsible for all the behavior of all of the children, but these agencies are charged with the responsibility of educating the young. Interacting variables of the home, the neighborhood, the culture, and the society must be incorporated into educational design, since regardless of any pleas to the contrary, it is the educator who is held accountable for what children end up learning. When we try to avoid this accountability, other agencies are either selected or created to perform educational functions.

Educators must speak to taxpayers and legislators in terms of learning results and system impacts. When relating our accomplishments to our objectives, we should not only provide our academic results (areas such as reading ability, standardized test results, and occupational skills), but also speak to what happens to our learners when they become citizens (cf. Murray, 1984; House and Linne, 1986). Education is about getting results, and we should speak to those rather than talk only about processes for education such as teacher credentialing, class hours, course content, and computers. The results and consequences of educational efforts are becoming a matter of public record and public concern (cf. Finn, 1986). The processes and methods for education should be selected by the professional educator only after the partners in education—the citizens (who pay the bills), the learners, and the educators—have agreed on what should be accomplished, why, and to what extent.

Management of education may be viewed as the process for the identification and delivery of required results. Most authors view management as including planning, organizing, implementing, and controlling to meet specific objectives. The management of education is defined here as involving the same functions as a system approach— a two-part process that includes:

- identify, justify, and scope needs
- get from "what is" to "what should be" (or meet the needs).

The tool for identifying, justifying, and scoping needs is called <u>needs assessment</u>. The tool to be used after identifying and selecting needs is a six-step problem-solving process for the <u>planning</u> of that which must be accomplished for getting from "what is" to "what should be." This six-step process will assist in developing the requirements for the successful accomplishment of reducing or eliminating the selected needs:

(1) Identify (or verify) the priority needs and associated problems.

(2) Determine requirements to solve the problem and identify possible alternative solutions for meeting the needs.

(3) Select solution tactics and tools from options.

(4) Implement solutions, including the management and control of the selected strategies and tools.

(5) Evaluate performance effectiveness and efficiency based on the needs and the requirements identified previously.

(6) Revise any or all previous steps (at any time in the process) to assure that the educational system is responsive, effective, and efficient.

The manager, before using this problem-solving process (perhaps more accurately labeled a problem-resolution process) should identify, document, and justify the educational goals and objectives to be met and should also identify the priority problems to be resolved!

The importance of the needs assessment phase cannot be overemphasized. It is not enough to solve a problem. Identifying the right problem in the first place is the key to successful educational planning.

A hypothetical case-in-point: The State of Euphoria's legislature passed a bill, signed by the governor, requiring the public school year to be increased by 7%. Some discrepancies soon arose, such as the state's teacher and support contracts did not cover this additional time, and there were no additional funds appropriated for this increase. Through applying the six-step model to these gaps (not enough staff and funds) the Gullo School District was able to find ways and re-

sources to lengthen the school year as mandated. The staff and resources were obtained, scheduled and used. It wasn't long before the
teachers, plunging into the longer school year, realized that there was
no guide for exactly how to utilize the increased time. They and the
legislators had assumed the problem: not enough time in class to
learn, and more time would deliver more mastery. But they had not
realized that there is more to facilitating mastery than more classroom hours . . . there are learning objectives based on needs, individual learning styles to be considered, learning strategies, instructional design and delivery, and a host of other factors required to
measurably improve learner performance. Unprepared to properly
use the added time, the teachers labored as best they could, but the
evaluation data showed that the extra time-in-class did not result in
better mastery, higher completion rates of students, more placements in college or more jobs obtained than the two years previous.
By solving the "time" problem the district still did not solve the
learner success problem. The premature solution (more time in school)
did not relate to the underlying problems of in-class and in-life performance and success.

Needs assessment plus the above six-step problem-solving process
together form the basic process model for a system approach to
educational planning. Its use will help define and design an overall
educational system to achieve required outcomes based on needs.

Again, it should be emphasized that only planning is under discussion in this book. Management requires that one first plan what
to do before doing what was planned.

a description of the elements of a system approach to educational management

Following is a brief discussion of the two basic parts, or phases, of
this system approach management process model: (1) needs assessment and problem identification plus (2) problem solving. To understand each part, let's first turn to examine a framework which allows
us to identify the organizational elements which make up any
educational system.

There are five "organizational elements" which can describe any
school system, from a local school to a state or national system. The
next section describes how these five organizational elements will
assist us in identifying needs and selecting ways and means to meet
them.

The Organizational Elements Model (OEM): A Framework for Useful Planning and Management

The successful educational manager has to correctly relate what learners, educators, and schools use, do, accomplish, and deliver. A useful framework which relates all of the elements of successful education is called the Organizational Elements Model (OEM)[4] (Kaufman, 1982; Kaufman & Stone, 1983; Kaufman, 1987a). This model defines five elements which relate what educational organizations use and do with what they accomplish.

The Organizational Elements Model (OEM) provides a holistic framework for selecting and linking the various "units of analysis" for identifying needs, analyzing them, defining useful objectives, and then selecting effective and efficient interventions, in other words, applying a system approach.

DEFINING THE ORGANIZATIONAL ELEMENTS MODEL (OEM)

That which educational organizations use, do, and deliver may be identified, defined, and related. The OEM relates internal—inside the organization—and external—outside of the organization—resources and processes with three kinds of results. The five Organizational Elements (OEs) are Inputs, Processes, Products, Outputs, and Outcomes, and are defined in Table 2.1.

Planning an Educational System: Three Planning Domains— Middle, Comprehensive, and Holistic

The five Organizational Elements (OEs) allow us to identify further three domains of planning. In fact one may plan an educational system (or subsystem) at each one of these levels.

Middle-level planning relates to inputs, processes, and products, such as planning a curriculum in math, or developing a new building. Comprehensive planning is wider in scope, and includes inputs, processes, products, and outputs, such as the planning for an entire high school, or a system-wide curriculum where learning at all

---

[4]I was tempted to rechristen this model "the Educational Elements Model" in order to emphasize its applicability to education. I resisted in favor of attempting to call the reader's attention to the reality that educators, like other professionals, work in and for organizations; also the similarities between education and other agencies are quite extensive. We can learn from each other. This same model may be applied to all organizations.

TABLE 2.1 The Organizational Elements and their relationship to Organizational Efforts, Organizational Results, Societal Impact. Also shown are two varieties of results, internal and external. (A variation of this figure and the relationships among the organizational elements is provided in Figure 8.1.)

	INPUTS (raw materials)	PROCESSES (how-to-do-its)	PRODUCTS (en-route results)	OUTPUTS (the aggregated products of the educational system which are delivered or deliverable to society)	OUTCOMES (the effects of outputs in and for society and the community)
EXAMPLES	Ingredients, existing human and educational resources; existing needs, goals, objectives, policies, board regulations, laws, money, values, societal and community characteristics, quality of life.	Educational means, methods, procedures; "excellence programs;" voucher plans, in-service training; teaching; learning; meditating; managing.	Course completed; competency test passed; competency acquired; learner accomplishments; teacher accomplishments; the educational "building blocks."	Graduates; program completors; job placements; certified licensees; etc.	Self-sufficient, self-reliant, productive individual; socially competent and effective; contributing to self and to others; no addictive relationship to others or to substances; financial independence.
		INTERNAL (Organization)			EXTERNAL (Societal)
CLUSTER SCOPE	Organizational Efforts		Organizational Results		Societal Results/Impacts

levels is related. Holistic planning is the widest scope of all, and includes inputs, processes, products, outputs, and outcomes.

A holistic planning frame of reference would be appropriate for an entire district strategic plan which intends to be responsive to current and future societal realities and imperatives. This frame not only considers courses and activities, but also all of the linkages among (a) teachers' and learners' contributions, (b) school contributions, and finally (c) the contributions of each of these to society.

The three planning domains[5] and their relationship to the OEs are shown in Figure 2.1.

WHY SELECT ANY OF THE THREE LEVELS: MIDDLE, COMPREHENSIVE, OR HOLISTIC?

By selecting a level other than the holistic, for example, the middle level, one assumes that the accomplishment of these products (such as increasing mastery scores on math) will in fact lead to useful organizational results (e.g., increased graduation rates) and positive societal consequences (e.g., self-sufficient graduates). Likewise, limiting oneself to the comprehensive level assumes that these outputs (e.g., graduates) actually will lead to fully functioning citizens. These assumptions are risky at best. Selecting a narrow frame of reference requires the assumption that there will be successful links to the larger ones.

What are the risks of implementing an educational improvement intervention only to find that it was (a) ineffective, (b) inefficient, (c) destructive to individual and/or organizational performance? If one is willing to risk any or all three of these negative consequences, then the choice becomes simple: pick the easiest frame of reference (e.g., middle or comprehensive level), model or approach, which will allow one to move ahead. In reality, most educational organizations do not evaluate the effectiveness of interventions (such as a computer literacy program) beyond checking to see if the target population performed at or above criterion levels on performance assessment instruments: if an intervention meets its product-level objectives, then the program is counted a success, and the interventionists may blithely go on to their next activity.

The "excellent organizations" thrust has discouraged such a focus upon intervention "splinters" alone. By including that which organizations do and deliver—more holistic concerns (cf. Kaufman,

[5]These three domains could be labeled "alpha" level for planning which starts with outcomes, "beta" level for planning starting with outputs, and "gamma" level for planning which starts with products. A variation of this option has been offered in Kaufman & English, 1979.

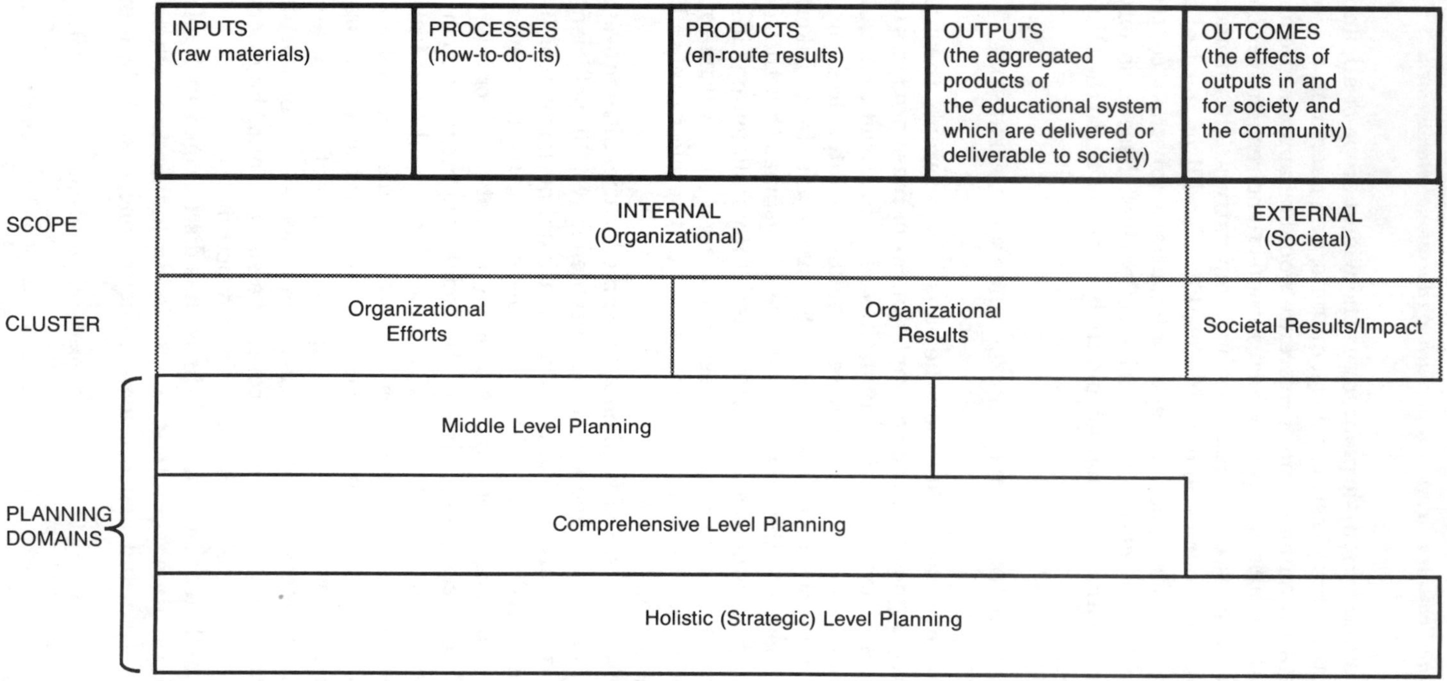

INPUTS (raw materials)	PROCESSES (how-to-do-its)	PRODUCTS (en-route results)	OUTPUTS (the aggregated products of the educational system which are delivered or deliverable to society)	OUTCOMES (the effects of outputs in and for society and the community)
INTERNAL (Organizational)				EXTERNAL (Societal)
Organizational Efforts		Organizational Results		Societal Results/Impact

SCOPE

CLUSTER

PLANNING DOMAINS

Middle Level Planning

Comprehensive Level Planning

Holistic (Strategic) Level Planning

Figure 2.1. Three planning domains as defined by the organizational elements they encompass.

1982; Kanter, 1983) and payoffs for clients—newer "excellence" management is starting to ask questions concerning how each educational component contributes to both the organizational productivity as well as client/societal good. Thus "deep change" (Kaufman & English, 1979), rather than cosmetic modifications, becomes possible, feasible, and justifiable. (Such a linking is suggested later in a "results chain" presented in Figure 2.4.) Rather than simply focusing on a part of an organization's problems, approaches such as the one presented here help draw attention to basic causes, problems and opportunities. For example, some organizational development approaches seek to determine "climate" of the operation, and attend only to people's feelings about current activities. This part-of-the-problem/part-of-the-organization concentration will often lead to fixing symptoms rather than dealing with basic causes. As H. Ross Perot (the successful computer and business entrepreneur) noted: "If the leaves of the bush are turning yellow, I'm not going to learn much studying yellow leaves. There's probably something wrong in the root system—not enough water, not enough fertilizer and some parasites on the trunk" (quoted in *Newsweek*, Nov., 1986).

But the choice of the unit of analysis for planning is optional. In some cases where considerable barriers exist, one could select a unit of analysis for change which will allow progress and set the stage for later more holistic planning and development. (Sooner or later, however, the societal consequences will come into play, either indirectly as a result of our being non-responsive, or because our rational thinking leads us back to viewing our educational system as a subsystem of society.)

ACCOUNTING FOR THE DYNAMIC NATURE OF EDUCATION

An educational enterprise is dynamic, not linear or lock-step. Activities and their results flow back and forth within the educational system, and this becomes comprehensible within the OEM framework. That which educational agencies use (inputs) are applied to doing things (processes) which have results (products, outputs, and outcomes). Sometimes a result is used as an input to another process which builds still another product. Next, many products may be combined into a result which the school can or does deliver to its community (output). Finally these delivered outputs have consequences for the graduates and their society (outcomes). This is a continuing, dynamic, interacting set of means and ends, as any educator realizes. How we manage this will determine the suitability of our methods, means and contributions. A limited hypothetical example is shown in Figure 2.2.

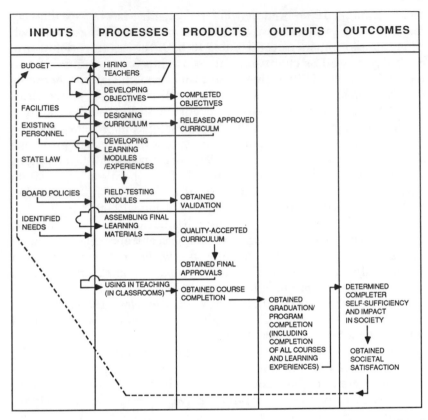

INPUTS	PROCESSES	PRODUCTS	OUTPUTS	OUTCOMES

Figure 2.2. The OEM may be used to visualize the dynamic nature of organizational efforts, results, and their consequences. There are back and forth flows between and within organizational elements as an educational agency applies resources, expends effort and obtains results. Also displayed is the impact these have within and outside the organization. Only a portion of a very complex curriculum-based example, is shown.

Using the OEM as a Practical Planning and Management Frame of Reference

An educational plan is a blueprint showing what must be accomplished to get from the current state of affairs to desired ones—to move from "what is" to "what should be." The five Organizational Elements (OEs) define the elements of any plan: inputs are used in the doing of educational processes which, in turn, deliver products. While products (e.g., passing a course in driver education, scoring at the 47th percentile on the SAT) may fulfill parts of the completion requirements, they are not by themselves sufficient for graduation. Products, then, must be collected together to form outputs (e.g., being certified for graduation). Finally, the accountable educational manager is interested in knowing the extent to which completers are successful in life, after schooling has been completed or terminated (the outcomes).

It is possible to use predictive societal indicators (Butz, 1983) to identify behaviors and results while a learner is in school which forecast societal consequences. Such indicators might include graffiti, truancy, property damage, arrests, student activities and responsibilities, and learning accomplishments.

PLANNING TO GET FROM "WHAT IS" TO "WHAT SHOULD BE":
ENTER INDUCTIVE LOGIC

Management of the educational enterprise requires that the system move from current results to desired ones. To help plan this, the five OEs may be formed into two tiers, one for "what is" and the other for "what should be."

In using the two-tiered OEM model for the first time, it might be simpler to first identify "What Is" for each Organizational Element, and then determine "What Should Be" for each. The two-tiered OEM is shown in Figure 2.3. A suggested first time operational sequence involves moving from What Is for Inputs, to Processes, to Products, then Outputs, and Outcomes. Then, using inductive logic, moving into the dimension of What Should Be from Outcomes through the remaining Elements to Inputs.

By including a "what should be" dimension in planning, an inductive aspect is added. If one were to confine planning to "what is" considerations alone, she or he would be improving current efficiency in achieving here-and-now organizational and societal purposes. By adding the "what should be" dimension, the opportunity to identify a better future set of outcomes is possible. Inductive thinking and activity are required when looking to "what should (or could) be" and the identification of possible better futures come into consideration.

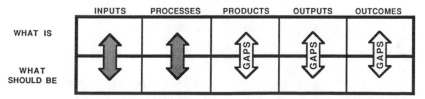

Figure 2.3. The OEM as a two-tiered (what is and what should be) framework.

It is this "what should be" consideration which is often missing from "excellence" and "Japanese management" initiatives.

It is important to use both levels (what is and what should be) in order to identify, define and document the gaps in results. It is from this data base that needs are identified.

NEEDS ASSESSMENT AND NEEDS ANALYSIS

Using the information from the two-tiered OEM, it is clear that one should first identify a need before analyzing it. Not doing so might risk focusing on "what should be" without knowing "what is." Three types of Needs Assessments may be conducted, one each for identifying and justifying the gaps between What Is and What Should Be for Outcomes, Outputs, and Products. Each time a need has been identified, one may analyze it—determine where the need comes from, and uncover its characteristics. Needs analysis breaks down previously identified needs to determine their origins and bases, usually relating inputs and processes to products.

defining and correctly linking the various units of analysis

Finding the "Right" Unit of Analysis:
Breaking the Splinter Orientation

Several "units of analysis"—the unit of change one utilizes in selecting and designing educational activities—are possible (Kaufman, 1983):

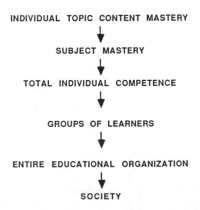

INDIVIDUAL TOPIC CONTENT MASTERY

↓

SUBJECT MASTERY

↓

TOTAL INDIVIDUAL COMPETENCE

↓

GROUPS OF LEARNERS

↓

ENTIRE EDUCATIONAL ORGANIZATION

↓

SOCIETY

What is the "right" unit of analysis? Attempts at improving educational effectiveness, efficiency, and impact have too often been limited to a portion of the whole concern: usually a splinter of total educational performance, such as a single skill, subject area, or course of study (Figure 1.1). Because of this narrow focus, available educational planning and improvement approaches and techniques tend (sadly) only to focus on one or two important parts of a total educational system. While such tools may be useful if one does not care about total organizational effectiveness and contribution, they tend not to integrate each "learning performance splinter" into an overall, cohesive framework, designed to deliver both educational and societal payoffs (Figure 1.2).

The recommended unit of analysis is the holistic (or strategic) frame of reference because it encompasses individual subject matter skills, a content area, the entire individual, groups of learners, the educational organization, and societal consequences. The holistic referent considers the impact each performance part makes in and for its portion of educational effectiveness. It also is concerned with the consequences of that which the organization delivers outside of itself: to be useful to and for society (cf. Kaufman, 1982; Kaufman and Stone, 1983; Carter, 1983; Kanter, 1983). The holistic unit of analysis considers all of the "splinters" and the ways in which they might be best selected, bundled, integrated, and applied to produce success within and external to the organization. By considering the societal requirements for success along with the total organization and all of its parts, it encourages the correct linking of means and ends.

Educational agencies are systems. As such, a change in any part of the organization has implications for all the other parts as well as for the whole. Useful holistic planning will better assure that changes in any part of the educational system will have payoffs throughout and for the entire system.

In order to relate educational efforts, educational results, and societal consequences, an appropriate "unit of analysis" for change must be selected. Too small a unit of analysis will yield changes which, while effective in part of an organization, may not make a system-wide contribution.

Putting the Organizational Elements Model (OEM) to Work

One way of linking the Organizational Elements for any organization is through the use of a hierarchy, or "results chain" among organizational levels and concerns (Figure 2.4).

Each hierarchical level should attempt to achieve a "fit" with the other levels to ensure educational effectiveness and efficiency. In other words, the results at any one level (such as mastery of English

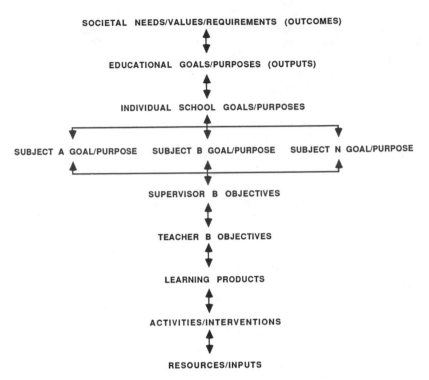

Figure 2.4. What educational organizations use, do, accomplish, and deliver should be integrated and related towards a common external impact (based, in part, on Kaufman, 1985). The results accomplished at any level and at each level (e.g., Subject A, Subject B, Teacher A) should lead to the successful results at all other levels.

grammar) should contribute to the results at all other levels (e.g., passing competency examinations, graduating, getting a job, being self-sufficient and successful societal functioning).

This hierarchy and its interrelationships show who is accountable for what, and provide a blueprint for the delegation of authority and responsibility. Any intervention, at any level, should emphasize and define the skills and abilities required of each and also specify exactly how each level will be integrated and related one to the others. By assuring that the results at each level will lead to those at all other levels, the appropriate meshing of results is better accomplished.

Sooner or later, each of the parts should relate to the whole organization, and the organization should make a positive contribution in and for society or it will likely fail, or be replaced. Regardless of the level of activity or assignment, the organization operates in five different but related areas, one for each of the five Organizational Elements.

ALLOCATION OF FUNCTIONS, THE EDUCATIONAL COMMUNITY, AND
EDUCATIONAL SUCCESS

Not everyone in the organization is capable of planning relative to Outcomes. Each person has her or his own assignment and responsibilities, but it is also important that each one's efforts and results be complementary and achieve relevant results. Thus, each of the educational elements should fit together, not work independently of each other and the organization, or independently of the survival and self-sufficiency of the learners and society as a whole.

A sensible allocation of functions to specific people and resources—who does what, to whom, and when—in an organization is practical and desirable. Each element (those involved people, resources, and their contributions) may check, at least, with the element next to it to assure that it is delivering things which are useful. By so doing, consistency and coordination between efforts and results may be better assured:

INPUTS ◄► PROCESSES ◄► PRODUCTS ◄► OUTPUTS ◄► OUTCOMES

The general assignments of educational personnel to each organizational element, with prime concern noted in **bold**, are depicted in Figure 2.5.

Teachers:	**INPUTS**
	PROCESSES
	PRODUCTS
Supervisors:	INPUTS
	PROCESSES
	PRODUCTS (for several teachers)
Principals:	INPUTS
	PROCESSES
	PRODUCTS
	OUTPUTS
Executive Senior-Managers (Central office staff, superintendents, board members):	PRODUCTS
	OUTPUTS
	OUTCOMES

Figure 2.5. Educational levels, associated personnel, concern, and focus upon the Organizational Elements. Organizational Elements which are in bold type are the primary concern of that professional.

Principals can assure the results flowing from their schools. Supervisors can assure only compliance with assignments and the efficiency of the work assigned to teachers in order to reach learning objectives. Executive senior educational managers can assure the effectiveness of the entire organization. They may determine current and future impact, and affirm or change policy relative to educational effects outside of the educational boundaries.

Linking organizational efforts, organizational results, and educational payoffs in and for society will allow any educational organization to:

- determine gaps between current and desired internal and external results
- determine where in the organization needs exist
- set priorities among these needs
- select the gaps of highest priority to close
- prepare objectives for closing the priority needs
- identify causes and origins of the needs
- identify and select the best methods and means to close the gaps
- determine the effectiveness and efficiency of the methods and means selected to meet the needs

management of education: an interim summary

Education is successful insofar as professionals and staff design, develop, and deliver learning experiences which allow learners to grow, develop, perform, and then apply what they have mastered both in school and life. Learners have a role in this success by becoming active participants in the learning process.

Management is the process of orchestrating educational efforts, educational results, and positive societal consequences. The OEM framework allows any planner or manager to conceptually relate that which educators use, do, accomplish and deliver to learners and society. The following section continues by providing an overview of the planning tools and methods for defining educational requirements based upon the identified and documented needs, so that educators may relate curriculum and teaching methods to the needs—finding solutions which will work.

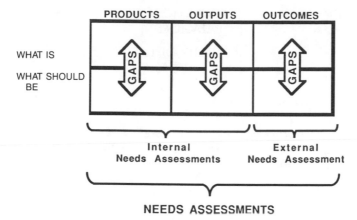

Figure 2.6. Three types of needs assessments. (These could also be labeled as "outcome-level," "output-level," or "product-level" needs assessments. Or another referent could be "alpha," "beta," and "gamma" level.)

finding the right planning level (and tools to use at the right place)

Identifying, Defining, Scoping, and Selecting Needs

Needs assessment assists us to define and select where we are going, why we are going there, and how to know when we have arrived. It assists us to identify, define, scope, justify, and select needs. Needs are gaps in results (products, outputs, outcomes), not gaps in means (inputs or processes).

Because there are three types of results—products, outputs, and outcomes—there are three types of needs assessments (see Figure 2.6).

QUALITY OF LIFE FACTORS

Self-sufficiency and self-reliance are critical. Without them, survival is not assured. But after these have been obtained, or their accomplishment is in the process of happening, the quality of that life becomes of central importance.

When planning, it is often all too convenient to overlook the quality of individual life. The temptation must be overcome, thus the addition of two elements to the OEM "template" for system planning is recommended:

SELF-SUFFICIENCY
FACTORS

QUALITY OF LIFE
FACTORS

More on this in Chapter 3.

EDUCATIONAL PARTNERS FOR A NEEDS ASSESSMENT

There are three types of human partners who should participate in a needs assessment:

- learners
- educators
- community and society members

By including those who may be, directly or indirectly, affected by any changes, they are more likely to "buy in" to the results. Drucker (1973) called this "transfer of ownership" when others come to "own" or "internalize" a change or situation through participation in defining and acquiring it.

THE HUMAN PARTNER GROUPS USE PERCEPTION AND
EXPERIENCE: "SOFT" DATA

Each partner group identifies gaps between current results and desired ones, and places the gaps, or needs, in priority order. These gaps are based upon each person's perceptions or experiences, and thus this type of resulting data is termed "soft" or "needs sensing" data. Then, each partner group comes to agreement with the others about the perceived needs and priorities.

INCLUDING ACTUAL, OBSERVED, PERFORMANCE: "HARD" DATA

There is one more "partner," not a human one, but actual performance data. While any one's perceptions are, for them, reality, another source of needs data is crucial: actual "hard" data, based upon controlled observations. The needs assessment process is aided by the collection and formal use of actual performance data, such as numbers of graduates and completers, job placements, entries into higher education, dropouts and pushouts, arrests, levels of self-sufficiency. "Hard" data is independently verifiable.

Increasingly, educational legislation and missions include the requirement for learners to be self-sufficient. The definition of self-sufficiency suggested (cf. Kaufman & Carron, 1980; Kaufman & English, 1979; Kaufman, 1982; Kaufman & Stone, 1983) is the condition where the learner is not under the care, custody or control of another person, agency, or substance.

COMBINING "HARD" AND "SOFT" DATA

When doing a needs assessment, the perceptions of the partners plus the performance data should be used to:

(1) Identify needs
(2) Agree upon the needs
(3) Select the needs to be met
(4) Place the selected needs in priority order

Each of the partners has a role, individually and together, in identifying the needs to be addressed (see Figure 3.2 in Chapter 3). Of course, needs are identified for the OEs of product, output, and outcome.

There are ten general steps in doing a needs assessment, which we shall list and explain in Chapter 3.

getting from "what is" to "what should be"

Once the needs have been identified, attention must next be given to developing a responsive plan for meeting the needs—closing the gaps between "what is" and "what should be."

A six-step problem-solving process is useful here. A detailed discussion of the tools for doing each step can be found in Chapters 5 and 6; the following sets the stage for that information.

Step 1—Identify (or Verify) Problems Based Upon Documented Needs

Earlier, educational needs were defined as measurable discrepancies between a current set of results and a required or desired set of results. An example of such a (hypothetical) need at the product level might be:

> Learners in the Steffy School District have a mean reading score of 32nd percentile and a standard deviation of 7 on the Utopian Valid Test of Reading Achievement. The district school board has required that the learners perform at the 50th percentile or better with a standard deviation not to exceed 5 on the Utopian Valid Test of Reading Achievement before June 13.

This example shows a measurable discrepancy between "what is" and "what should be," at the product-level (see Table 2.1), namely, of a mean score difference of 18 and a standard deviation of 5. This stating of a need as a gap defined in measurable performance terms, such as suggested by Mager (1975), or Popham (1966), is a critical feature of system planning. Doing so provides a tangible, quantified starting referent for the design of a responsible educational system. It also provides the criteria which will let you know when you have met the need or closed the gap. A statement of need describes results gaps and therefore must be free of any solutions or "how-to-do-its." [In reality, it would have been preferable if the Steffy School District had been using criterion-referenced assessment instruments in order that actual individual performance discrepancies, rather than group- (or norm) referenced ones, could have been identified.]

In some cases the needs will have already been assessed, identified, documented, and selected. When this information is available, this first step requires the planner to review that data and assure its timeliness and accuracy before moving on. When one simply has to check the needs assessment data base, then, it becomes a matter of verifying the needs.

Step 2—Determine Solution Requirements and Alternatives

The needs assessment process has identified discrepancies for resolution on the basis of priority and has provided overall requirements for an educational system. These overall requirements serve as the "mission objective and performance requirements" for system planning and later design. By comparing this statement of the problem with the situations and results currently experienced, the system planner can find out where the system is going and how to tell when it has arrived.

Having used the statement of needs to describe both the current situation and the success they seek, the educational manager and the educational system planner must decide on the requirements to resolve the problems they face.[6] Using educational "system analysis," they can determine system requirements and possible solution strategies and tools in layers or levels of details from the most general to the most specific.

This management step and its associated tools does not select how to solve the problem(s), but rather determines what function is to be

[6]Some authors might call this "needs analysis."

accomplished and what alternative strategies and tools are available to accomplish each requirement. Planning for the selection of the "hows" occurs in the system analysis step.

The steps and tools of educational system analysis include:

(1) Mission analysis.

(2) Function analysis.

(3) Methods-means analysis.

These are described in greater detail in Chapters 4 through 7. They form a process for determining feasible requirements for educational system design.

The system analysis process is designed to determine the feasible "whats" for system planning and design by analyzing requirements and identifying possible alternatives in successive levels of increasing detail.

Let's take a closer look at these tools of system analysis, for each contribute a little more to the determination of (1) what is required to meet the identified need (gap), (2) what alternatives are available to achieve each requirement, and (3) what the advantages and disadvantages are of each alternative solution possibility.

First, the tools for determining the requirements for getting from where we are to where we should be are mission and function analysis. Both help us to ascertain what is to be accomplished to meet the need, but not how. The mission analysis tells us about requirements for the total problem resolution and function analysis tells about more detailed aspects of each part of that problem. The use of these tools has been likened to looking through a microscope with lenses of increasing magnification (Corrigan and Kaufman, 1966). The first lens (mission analysis) gives us the big picture, and the second lens (function analysis) shows us a smaller part of the total problem in greater detail.

After we have identified all the parts of this system, we can identify possible methods and means (or tactics and tools) for each of the requirements we have unearthed during mission and function analysis—we match requirements against possible solutions and note the relative advantages and disadvantages of each so that we can later pick the best ones for solving our problem.

As we look at the individual tools presented in this chapter, and as we see them again in greater detail in the following chapters, we might think of them as peeling back layers of an onion—we go deeper and deeper into the "core" and find out more about how the whole is put together.

MISSION ANALYSIS

Proceeding from the needs assessment and problems delineation, the mission analysis states the overall goals and measurable performance requirements (criteria) for the achievement of required results. The mission objective and its associated performance requirements state the appropriate specifications for the system being planned and designed.

The next part of mission analysis is the statement of a management plan (called a mission profile) showing the "major" milestones or the central pathway for solving a given problem. An example of such a management plan, a possible mission profile for preparing instructional materials (if the mission is just that product level problem), is presented in Figure 2.7.

(Actually to show that each function is a product, the wording of each technically could show actual accomplishment, e.g., in Figure 2.7, Function 2.0 "Determined detailed. . . ." For ease of communication and to emphasize that mission profiles identify products to be delivered, however, such changes will not be shown in this and other examples.)

It is interesting to note that the overall process model for problem resolution may also be shown as a mission profile. Such a profile, containing a management plan for identifying and resolving problems in a logical, orderly manner, is shown in Figure 2.8.

Flow charts like those in Figures 2.7 and 2.8 provide a graphic display of a system, its components, and subsystems relationships in a simple, "at-a-glance" format. A flow chart, which identifies functions (or things to be accomplished) and their interrelations, may be read by following the solid lines and connecting arrows and by noting the order of the numbers. (Details of flow chart construction and interpretation are presented in Chapter 5.)

Mission analysis, then, is the system analysis step that reveals: (1) what is to be achieved, (2) what criteria will be used to determine success, and (3) what are the steps (functions) required to move one from the current situation to the desired state of affairs. The steps and tools of mission analysis are:

1. What is the system to accomplish and what criteria will be used to determine success?

1. Mission objective and performance requirements.

2. What are the basic steps or milestone results required to be completed in order to get one from where one is to where one should be?

2. Mission profile.

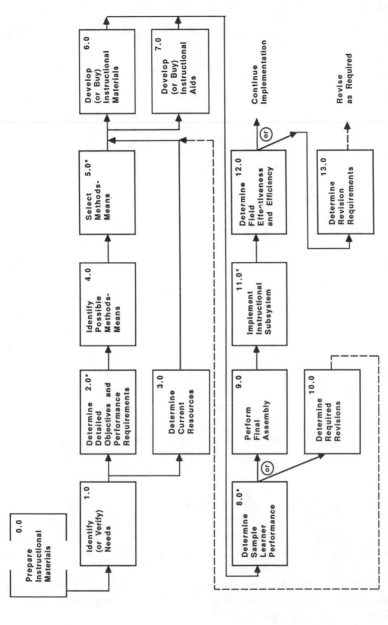

Figure 2.7. A possible mission profile for a "product" level function requiring instructional materials. All other functions could actually interact with all other functions, so not all "feedback" or revision pathways are identified. An asterisk indicates a possible point for obtaining management approval before proceeding.

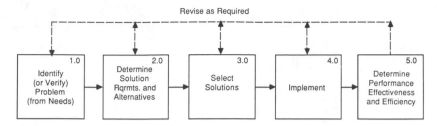

Figure 2.8. A general problem-solving process shown in flow chart form. Five of the six steps are identified and numbered; the last (revise as required) is indicated by broken lines to note that revision may take place at any problem-solving step.

FUNCTION ANALYSIS

The mission profile has provided the basic functions, or milestones, that delineate the major "things" that must be performed. The next part of an educational system analysis is to identify and define <u>what</u> is to be accomplished to get each one of the milestones in the mission profile accomplished.

Function analysis is the process for determining requirements and subfunctions for accomplishing each element in the mission profile. As such, it may be considered a vertical expansion of the mission profile.

Again, as was true for the mission objectives, each function in the mission profile will have performance requirements, and a "miniature" mission profile may be constructed to describe the functions that will get one from "what is" to the accomplishment of each mission profile function. This increasingly detailed analysis of functions and subfunctions is illustrated in Figure 2.9, which depicts a hypothetical function analysis of a mission profile function of "identify problem –," the first function in the generic six-step problem-solving process model.

The vertical expansion, or analysis, is continued through the function level until units of performance are identified (rather than collections of things to be done which are, again arbitrarily, called <u>functions</u>). The identification of the lowest order of functions occurs when one could not break them down any further without having to say "how" each would be accomplished. This most finite level of function identification and ordering is the last "breaking-down" step of an educational system analysis.

Note that each level of a function analysis carries a number identifying the level of analysis. Function analysis, furthermore, may (and usually does) consist of several levels.

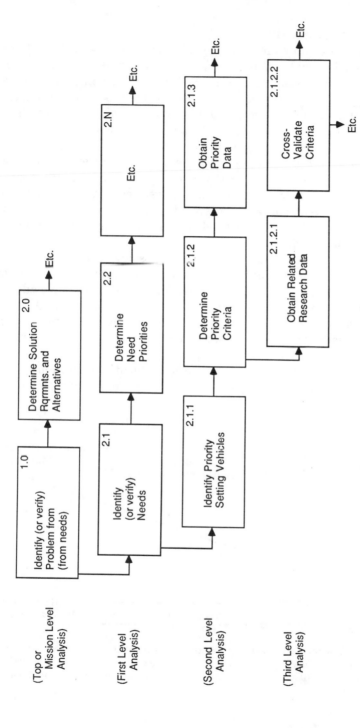

Figure 2.9. An example of a hypothetical function analysis showing the manner in which any functions may be analyzed into lower level constituent functions. This is only a partial analysis and each level's incompleteness is noted by "etc."

METHODS-MEANS ANALYSIS

Recalling that an educational system analysis is a tool for determining feasible "whats" for problem solution and that the second step in a problem-solving process is "Determine Solution Requirements <u>and Solution Alternatives</u>," let us briefly look at the remaining step of a system analysis—the identification of possible methods and means (or tactics and tools) for achieving each of the performance requirements or group of performance requirements.

The methods-means analysis may be conducted after mission and function analyses have been completed, or it may be conducted in parallel with each of them as the analysis of additional requirements progresses from level to level. Figure 2.10 shows a "process diagram" for conducting a methods-means analysis in such a parallel (or ongoing) fashion.

A methods-means analysis identifies possible tactics and tools available for achieving each performance requirement or family of performance requirements and additionally lists the relative advantages and disadvantages of each to assist in later selection. Also, as noted in great detail later, a methods-means analysis will provide an ongoing feasibility study in that it will indicate, at each stage, if there exist any tactics and tools to meet requirements.

Methods-means analysis, like the other educational system analysis steps, determines <u>what</u> is to be done (what possibilities exist

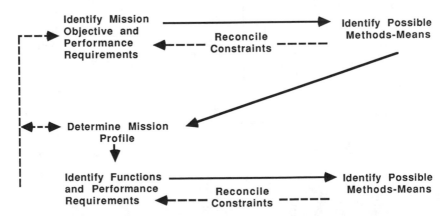

Figure 2.10. The relationship among the steps of a system analysis process. Note that a continuing feasibility check is being made in order to determine if there are any methods-means available for accomplishing each function and its associated performance requirements.

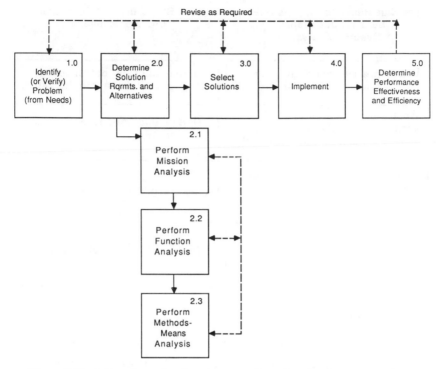

Figure 2.11. A flow chart showing the steps of an educational system analysis.

in the case of methods-means analysis) and <u>not how</u> it is to be accomplished.

system analysis summary

The steps and tools of an educational system analysis determine the feasible "whats" of problem solution. The tools of analysis and synthesis are used in determining requirements for system design. Again referring to the generic process model for educational management utilizing a system approach, needs assessment and system analysis both deal with "what," and the balance of the model is concerned with "how." Figure 2.11 shows the relation between problem-resolution and the steps of system analysis.

Restating the system analysis process, Figure 2.12 displays ques-

The Questions to Be Answered by an Educational System Analysis	The Steps in an Educational System Analysis
Where are we going and how do we know when we've arrived?	Derive mission objectives and performance requirements.
What are the things that will keep us from where we're going and how do we eliminate them?	Derive and reconcile constraints.
What are the major milestones along the way to where we're going?	Derive mission profile.
What are the "things" that must be completed to get each milestone accomplished?	Perform function analysis.
What are the possible ways and means for getting the "things" done?	Perform methods-means analysis.

Figure 2.12. The questions to be answered in an educational system analysis and each one's relation to the steps of performing that analysis.

tions to be answered in an educational system analysis and relates these to the steps of an educational system analysis.

problem resolution

By completing steps 1.0 and 2.0 of problem-resolution one has planned what has to be accomplished to define what the system must deliver, and what are the alternative ways and means available to complete the mission. The following steps allow for planning to actually accomplish the mission.

Step 3—Select Solutions (Tactics and Methods) from Among Options

This step begins the "how-to-get-it-done" portion of the system planning process. Here the appropriate tools and tactics for achieving the various requirements are selected. Frequently a choice criterion of "cost-results" (cf. Levin, 1983; Kaufman and Stone, 1983) is used, that is, the selection from among options which will at least achieve the minimal requirements at the lowest cost. All too frequently, educators begin the system design procedure at this point—without the specific delineation of problems and requirements—and select the methods and means on the basis of professional judgment or on a mere assumption of the problems and the requirements.

Selecting methods and means from options requires that the various identified functions and tasks be allocated to: (1) people, (2) things, and/or (3) people and things in combination.

Selection must be made on the basis of the system as a whole, noting the interactional characteristics of the various requirements of the system. Frequently, tools (see Chapter 7) called "systems analysis" methods (such as modeling and simulation) are utilized to determine the most effective and efficient means of meeting the requirements. By simulation, different methods and tactics can be "tried out" in a fashion that will not compromise the current, ongoing educational activity.

Step 4—Implement (Solution Tactics and Methods)

It is at the fourth step that the products of planning and selection are to be actually accomplished. The methods and means are obtained, designed, adapted, or adopted. A management and control subsystem is developed to assure that everything will be available and utilized as required and that proper data will be collected to determine the extent to which the system is functioning as required. The system, based upon the plan, is put into operation, including all the complexities of utilization and acquisition of people, equipment, learners, facilities, budgets, and the many other factors necessary for a properly functioning educational system.

Step 5—Determine Performance Effectiveness and Efficiency

Data are to be collected concerning both the process and the products of the system during and after the system's performance. Against the requirements established in the needs assessment and the derived detailed determination of requirements obtained from the system analysis, performance of the system is to be compared with these intended results: evaluation. Discrepancies are noted between actual system performance and the performance requirements, providing data on what is to be revised and thus giving diagnostic information that will permit valid system revision.

Step 6—Revise System as Required

Based on the performance of the system as indicated by the performance data, any or all previous steps may be modified and the system redesigned, if necessary. This self-correctional feature assures constant relevance and practicality. An educational system is never considered to be complete, for it must be constantly evaluated in terms of:

(1) Its ability to identify and then meet the needs and requirements to which it set out to respond.

(2) The continued appropriateness of the original needs and requirements. Thus we must have not only internal consistency and performance, but constant checking of needs and requirements to assure external validity—that everything works in the outside world as well.

some assumptions

This paradigm of a system planning approach to education is a management process that is intended to be rational, logical, orderly, systematic, and self-correcting. It requires that the planner/analyst/manager be open and objective and that only valid data be used in the planning, implementation, and evaluation. The following assumptions are included:

(1) A system approach to educational problem identification and resolution will result in effectiveness and efficiency measurably greater than any other presently available process yields.

(2) Educators are charged with the responsibility of intervening in people's lives: we should make certain that what they are doing will be useful.

(3) Needs, attitudes, wants, and values can be specified in (or at least indicated by) measurable performance terms.

(4) It is better to try to state the existence of something and attempt to quantify it than it is to proclaim it as nonmeasurable and leave its existence and accomplishment still in question.

(5) There is frequently a difference between hope and reality.

(6) Teaching does not necessarily equal learning.

(7) Educational areas that seem to defy quantification in system planning offer prime areas for efforts in educational research.

(8) A self-correctable system approach has greater utility than an open-loop process (which does not check its utility outside of itself) for achieving responsive education.

(9) No system approach procedure is ever the ultimate system. A system approach, like any other tool, should be constantly challenged and evaluated relative to other alternatives and should be revised or rejected when other tools or approaches prove more responsive and useful.

(10) While no approach can completely protect itself from misuse or misapplication, this approach will, more frequently than others, deliver results which are useful in the worlds outside education. That which is presented here is based upon lawful application and constitutionally-founded societal purposes.

usefulness of a system approach

If an educational manager desires to plan and design an education system without prejudging the adequacy of the current system, this model of a system approach can be valuable—it does not automatically imply that the entire current system is wanting, and thus special precautions must be taken to assure that those portions of the educational system which are meeting the requirements are not discarded in the change process.

A system approach to education is a potentially useful tool for the educator who is willing to make the assumption that the overall job of an educational manager/administrator is to identify and solve educational problems in the most relevant and practical manner possible.

System analysis, as we have noted, consists of a set of planning tools which reveals <u>what</u> is to be accomplished to meet identified and documented needs. Mission and function analyses identify requirements for accomplishment; methods-means analysis identifies possible solution tactics, methods, and tools.

At the completion of system analysis, the planner has identified and developed a plan for all of the feasible "whats" for problem solution, and he knows the possible ways and means for achieving each "what."

Finally, we must also remember that the usefulness of any system approach lies in (a) the validity of the data it uses and (b) the objectivity and integrity of the planner.

summary: system analysis, system approach, and planning

A system approach, as described here, is a two-phase process which uses needs assessment to identify and define important needs, and a six-step process for planning for the realizing of the necessary, valid planned change.

The functions involved in needs assessment, as well as the problem-solving six steps are quite general, and a self-correcting process is built into the approach. Thus the educator has a "road map" for planning for achievement of the desired change. Problem solving may be used at each step of the process, and in fact is used to plan each step of a new educational program or to redesign an existing one.

There have been a lot of concepts, models, and labels introduced in this chapter. The pieces discussed relate thus:

SYSTEM APPROACH

- assessing needs
- meeting needs

PLANNING REVEALS WHAT TO DO TO ACCOMPLISH EACH

using Needs Assessment data
    to
Prioritize problems

PLANNING FOR PROBLEM SOLUTION

- six step process
  uses
- system analysis to "determine solution requirements and identify solution alternatives"

The pieces fit together to form a system approach to educational planning using the tools described here.

USING THE OEM AND THE SIX-STEP PROCESS TOGETHER

There is a fit between these two tools. Each time one wishes to verify and eliminate a gap in any of the Organizational Elements, the six steps may be used. As may be seen in Figure 2.13, the six steps may be applied to any one, or any combination of the OEs.

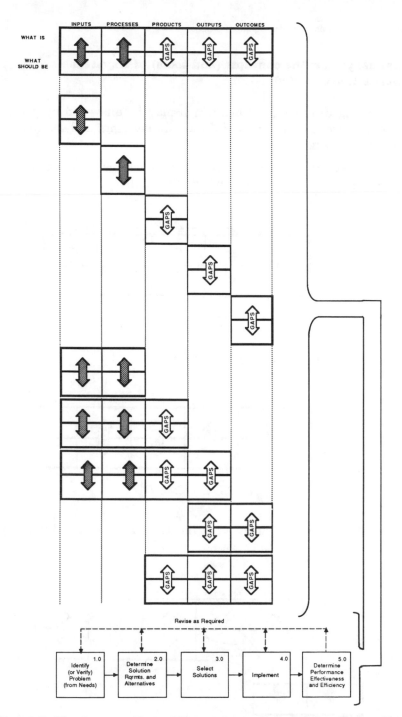

Figure 2.13. The six-step problem-solving process may be used to close the gaps identified in any of these practical combinations of the organizational elements.

summary: how the concepts (and tools) of a system approach are related

Following are five questions which may be answered by using a system approach. For each of these, the concepts and appropriate tools are shown.

(1) What are all the parts, activities, and actions of my educational organization . . . and what do they deliver?

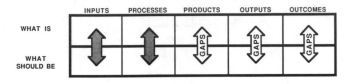

THE OEM

(2) What do I do to identify and document needs?

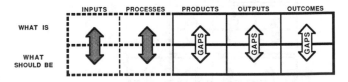

NEEDS ASSESSMENT

(3) What do I do to identify what has to be accomplished in order to get from "what is" to "what should be?"

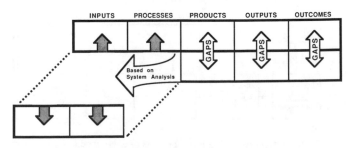

THE SIX-STEP PROBLEM-SOLVING PROCESS

(4) What do I use to determine the details of what has to be accomplished, along with possible ways and means to be used for each, in order to get from "what is" to "what should be?"

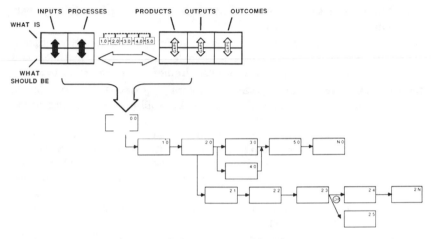

SYSTEM ANALYSIS

(5) After doing this planning, how do I translate all of this in order to design and deliver useful results?

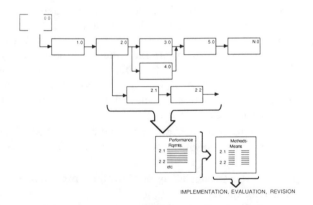

SYSTEM ANALYSIS & SYSTEM SYNTHESIS

The tools and techniques of needs assessment and system analysis are presented in detail in the chapters which follow.

glossary

Accountability   being held responsible for the delivery of required results along with the ability to show accomplishment of what one set out to do.

Closed-loop process   a process that is self-correcting based on its performance or nonperformance.

Constraint   anything that will make it impossible to accomplish a performance requirement. Only if there are no possible methods and means for achieving a performance requirement is a constraint evident.

Educational management (using a system approach)   a two phase process which includes: identifying, defining, scoping, and selecting needs; getting needs reduced or eliminated.

The primary process for identifying needs is called "needs assessment," and the process for developing plans for meeting the needs is a six-step problem-solving process that includes: identify (or verify) problem based on needs; determine solution requirements and alternative solutions; select solutions from among alternatives; implement selected tactics and tools; determine performance effectiveness and efficiency; revise as required, wherever required, whenever required.

Educational system planning   the use of a system approach for the identification of all requirements for identifying, justifying and meeting needs. It includes the use of the tools associated with needs assessment and system analysis. When it is completed all the requirements and an identification of possible solution alternatives for designing, implementing, and achieving a responsive (and successful) educational system are present.

Function analysis   the analysis of each of the elements (functions) in the mission profile, which shows what is to be done to complete each function. Function analysis is like a miniature mission analysis that is specific to a smaller part of the overall problem. Like the mission analysis, it includes performance requirements (specifications) for the successful accomplishment of each function in the mission profile. Function analysis, however, depicts the subfunctions in the order and relationship necessary to successfully accomplish each function.

Hard data   Independently verifiable data which have been derived from controlled observations of performance, status, condition, or actual consequences.

Management   a process consisting of planning, implementing, and controlling for meeting needs.

Methods-means analysis   the determination of possible methods and means (tactics and tools) for accomplishing each performance requirement, and a listing of the relative advantages and disadvantages of each.

Mission analysis the process of identifying for the problem selected the elements of: (1) where are we going; (2) what criteria we use to let us know when we have arrived; and (3) a management plan to show what functions must be performed to get us from where we are to where we have to be. This management plan is usually depicted in the form of a flow chart called a mission profile.

Open-loop process a process that does not self-correct on the basis of performance.

Organizational Elements Model (OEM) five organizational elements (inputs, processes, products, outputs, outcomes) identify and relate organizational efforts (inputs and processes), organizational results (products and outputs) and societal consequences (outcomes). The OEM is a two-tiered model for the dimensions of "what is" and "what should be."

Using the OEM, there are three levels of results-oriented planning and needs assessments possible: outcome level (or "alpha"), output level (or "beta"), product level (or "gamma").

Organizational Elements (OE) inputs, processes, products, outputs, outcomes.

Performance requirement a measurable specification for a result. There may be two types of performance requirements—one that tells what the end result will look like or do, and another type that identifies specifications that are "given" relative to the manner in which the result is to be produced.

Problem a documented discrepancy between current results and desired ones selected for resolution: a need chosen for resolution or reduction.

Problem-solving process six steps: identify (or verify) problem based on needs; determine solution requirements and solution options; select solution tactics and methods from among options; implement selected tactics and methods; determine performance effectiveness and efficiency; revise as required, wherever required, whenever required.

Quality of life factors that which makes life worth living, including beauty, poetry, art, music, dance, pleasant environment, happiness, relationships, etc.

Result any consequence of applying resources and a process. There are three types of results: products, outputs, and outcomes.

Self-sufficiency that point where an individual is not under the care, custody, or control of another person, agency, or substance. Self-sufficiency does include forming and maintaining personal and social relationships.

Soft data data based upon perceptions of individuals. A needs assessment using only this type of data is more accurately called "need sensing."

System analysis a set of related tools used for analyzing the requirements of a system that would, if satisfied, eliminate or reduce the identified need. The analysis identifies requirements (or specifications) for meeting the needs and the interrelations among the requirements; it also identifies potentially useful methods and means for meeting each requirement. The three related tools of system analysis are: mission, function, and methods-means analysis. These tools are used to define the requirements (and thus define the problem) in increasing levels of detail and refinement.

exercises

1. What is accountability?

2. What is a system approach as defined in this book?

3. What is the OEM? Define the OEs. Give an application and example of each OE in your school system.

4. The tools of educational system analysis are:

a. _____

b. _____

c. _____

5. In flow chart form, show the general (generic) six-step problem-solving process model described in this book.

6. An educational system planning procedure (a management process) must take the planner from _____ to _____ .

7. Show the relationship between needs assessment and the six-step problem-solving process.

8. What is the importance of the sixth step of the problem-solving process, "revise as required"?

9. A system approach, as described here, is a process for _____ _____ .

10. Why is a system approach suggested as a viable process for educational management?

CHAPTER 3

assessing educational needs[7]

TODAY, MUCH OF educational planning, curriculum improvement, and attention is given over to <u>solving</u> problems. We invest a lot of time and money in "hot problems," which have been identified by legislators, politicians, citizen groups, and others often searching for a quick fix to overt symptoms. Regardless of the political pressures to "do something quick," or "acceptable," it is at least as important to first identify and justify the real problems which provide the rational starting place for applying interventions and attempts to improve results (cf. Peddiwell, 1939). Problems are needs which have been selected for resolution. Before tackling them, it is important to assure ourselves that they are the right problems, and that we have convincing reassurance that resolving them will lead to both individual learner competence as well as desired educational success.

Needs assessments provide the direction for useful problem solving. They supply the necessary data to identify, document, and realistically prioritize important gaps in results, and thus allow the selection of appropriate problems. By first selecting important problems before rushing off to solve them, the effectiveness and efficiency of any educational planning and resulting operations may be improved. Needs assessments are discrepancy (not deficiency) analyses which identify and document gaps in results, not in resources or methods. They clearly allow planners to identify and document:

- What are our current results?
- What results should we get?

[7]In this chapter, and the ones following, words are used which are unique to the "Organizational Elements Model." This model is presented in detail in Chapter 2. Those not familiar with it, and the particular use of the terms inputs, processes, products, outputs, outcomes, organizational efforts, organizational results, societal impact, and needs assessment are encouraged to reread that chapter.

A practical needs assessment must have several characteristics:

(1) The data we collect and use must represent the actual world of learners, educators, and society, both as it exists now, and as it will, could, and should exist in the future.

(2) No needs assessment and problem determination is complete; we must realize that any statement of needs is tentative, and we should constantly question the validity of existing needs data, and revise as required.

(3) Needs data must relate only to gaps in results, never to gaps in inputs or processes (which are termed "quasi needs"). Since there are very important differences between needs and wants, and means and ends, this results-only orientation cannot be over-emphasized.

(4) Different partners (learners, educators, society) in educational planning have varying values, and these must be considered in any useful needs assessment. No matter how logical the list of needs, those who can and will be impacted by any change must agree that the needs are real and important to eliminate or reduce.

(5) The needs identified and selected must have the substantial agreement of the majority of the planning partners.

Since needs provide the rational basis for identifying where an educational system should be headed, and provide the basic data for planning, a no-nonsense needs assessment is fundamental to educational success. While it might be more conventional and convenient to ask planning partners about their wishes, or what solutions and resources they desire (needs sensing, solutions assessment, wish-lists), educational agencies are chartered to get results. The gap between current results and required ones has to be the basis for any rational approach to needs assessment.

nine recommended steps for doing a needs assessment

Planning rationally starts with needs assessment: determining where to go and why go there. Needs assessment is the first part of a system approach to planning. There are nine suggested basic steps (or functions) for doing a needs assessment:

- Decide to plan using data from a needs assessment.
- Select the needs assessment and planning level.

- Identify the needs assessment and planning partners.
- Obtain the planning partners' participation.
- Obtain planning partners' acceptance of the needs assessment and planning level.
- Collect needs data.
- List identified and documented needs.
- Place needs in priority order and reconcile disagreements.
- List and obtain agreement on the problems to be resolved.

Following is what is involved in each needs assessment step.

(1) Decide to Plan Using Data from a Needs Assessment

Planning is a substitute for good luck; doing a needs assessment is a substitute for good luck in determining where one should be going . . . and why. It is also a rational alternative to simply continuing that which we are doing now, regardless of how well or poorly we are performing.

As we noted earlier, a plan is a blueprint for action and results. It specifies functions (or products) to be completed to get from current results to desired ones. A plan derives from determining where to go and provides a justification of why to go there. The decision to plan using a needs assessment includes the commitment to being proactive and gaining control of the future. The commitments to proactive, results-oriented planning should be made by the planning partners, including those who will be affected by the results and those who will have to implement the plan.

Several key issues must be resolved at this step.

THE MEANS/ENDS ISSUES

Of critical importance is the commitment to attend to gaps in results only, not to allow the concern for methods, techniques, and resources to slip into the forefront. Many contemporary expeditions into so-called needs assessments (sometimes also termed "needs analysis," and "front-end analysis") really examine wishes, wants, and desires, usually concerning resources and methods. These approaches are popular, and since most people think in terms of a means-orientation, they (unfortunately) may have more initial appeal to educators and citizens alike. In fact, much legislation, usually well-meaning, is about means (hours of school, budgets, teacher credentialing, career ladders, etc.), and assumes that worthy results will follow. We know better (Kaufman, 1986a), but hope springs eternal, and the means-orientation seems to have a life of its own. We are still held accountable for results as well!

In education, it will be almost impossible to develop and evaluate any programs, projects, and interventions which begin with methods and end with techniques. While compliance is important to the reliability of an intervention (doing what one was supposed to do the way one was supposed to do it), the basic issue facing educators is getting results. Means include the resources and methods used to get results, and are only important to the extent to which the means are actually linked with achieving ends. Making the commitment to a needs assessment which considers only results—products, outputs, and/or outcomes—is essential.

THE "WHERE-DO-THE-NEEDS-COME-FROM" ISSUE

It is often tempting, in the name of saving time and trouble, to assign the needs assessment to a working group of the educational agency staff. While it is tidier for the job to be done internally, to do so risks not having the important input of all of the educational partners (educators, learners, and community), and also risks that the resulting products will not be accepted by all those affected when it comes time to implement the recommended changes. Get all the partners involved. The extra time and effort will be worth the investment at budget and implementation time.

THE "WE ALREADY KNOW WHAT WE 'NEED'" ISSUE

Most schools and districts have goals and objectives. Unfortunately these listed intentions usually have several features in common: (a) they deal with means, solutions, or approaches (e.g., learners will know their cultural heritage; learners will appreciate the importance of science in life); (b) they seem to cover the same territory (cf. The Ten Cardinal Principles; The Ten Proposed Goals of Education/Educational Testing Service, etc.); and (c) they were derived by local educator groups through a lot of hard work and give-and-take, so they won't let go of them easily. The existing goals and objectives may serve as a base for educational planning, but first they have to be converted to measurable objectives with performance indicators for measuring attainment. The doing of this will be covered later in this chapter.

In related fashion, many people really do believe they know what must be done (sex education/no sex education; evolution/creationism; graded schools/continuous progress; etc.) even without supporting data. These "needs," of course, are means or solutions, and should be put aside until the gaps in results are identified (illegitimate birth rate, drug convictions, student grades and completions, etc.). Such so-called "needs" may be written down and revisited later as possible alternative methods and means. The use of these "premature solutions" should be delayed until they may be objectively considered during the methods-means analysis (discussed in Chapter Six).

THE "OTHERS WILL TELL US WHAT TO DO" ISSUE

Educators tend to be reactors rather than being proactive. For years, others (school boards, legislators, Federal and state governments) have given us our orders which we have followed. Doing what others tell us to do has some seeming advantages: we don't have to think too much about our professional responsibilities; we can avoid blaming ourselves when things don't work out; we don't have to struggle to define and achieve our own destinies. In truth, regardless of who told us to do what, we are held responsible when things go awry . . . and they usually do. Education and educators have been blamed for such circumstances as low test scores, drug addiction, children having children, dropouts, and worker ineptitude and laziness. This blame comes to us even though others have mandated what we are to do, and how we are to do it. If we are not going to escape blame, why don't we take an active role in helping to decide what are the needs, and what are the best ways of eliminating them? By being proactive, we educators may better define where schools should be going, and how to best get there.

(2) Select the Needs Assessment and Planning Level: Middle, Comprehensive, or Holistic[8]

How much of the educational world should be considered and tackled? In terms of the OEM, which ones should be included? Three levels, or units of analysis, are possible:

- Middle level needs assessment and planning includes a focus on educational resources (inputs) plus the procedures and methods (processes) to be employed in activities plus the immediate results (products) accomplished. For example, this level of concern might be directed toward improving learner

[8]In other work, this has been termed "strategic" to note that it was the basic functional frame of reference to consider in making certain that planning would allow the organization and its clients to survive and make a contribution in today's and tomorrow's worlds.

mastery of 10th grade geometry from an average of 57% scoring at or above grade level now, to at least 80% scoring at or above grade level within two years. The accomplishment of this might involve teachers, computer-aided instruction, workbooks, and the funds to obtain and use them. The unit of analysis for the middle level is the course or program. This focus is only upon inputs, processes, and products.

- Comprehensive level needs assessment and planning includes the middle level (above) plus the associated accomplishments of an entire curriculum or educational program, such as not only requiring criterion performance level in geometry, but in all other required courses necessary for learners to be certified for graduation from high school (outputs).

The unit of analysis for this "comprehensive" level is the total organization: inputs, processes, products, and outputs. It is made up of that which a school system uses, does, and delivers both to itself as well as to external clients, society, and community. For example, using necessary personnel (e.g., teachers and aides) and resources (classrooms, teaching aids, media support, etc.) in order to deliver learner competence in geometry is combined with competence in all other required courses and activities in order to meet district graduation requirements.

- Holistic (or strategic) level needs assessment and planning includes the comprehensive level (above) plus a consideration of the usefulness of the organization's contributions—its graduates and completers—to the world in which its learners must function after completion (outcome). The unit of analysis for the holistic level includes inputs, processes, products, outputs, and outcomes.

This level includes anything an organization uses, does, and delivers, as well as the impact these have in and for clients (including society). Continuing the geometry course example, the combination of competent completers of all of the required courses plus the use of appropriate means (e.g., educational materials, methods and resources, etc.) leading to graduation should result in an increased number of graduates who will be self-sufficient, self-reliant, and personally satisfied in the future. It is not enough to simply nod towards societal usefulness (such as employer satisfaction alone) but also to consider the payoffs the results have to others and our world—being "good neighbors."

The specific factors to be included in needs assessment and planning depend upon the nature of each educational system's environment and requirements. As are the students in our schools, all educational systems are the same.

One may assess needs (and plan) at any of these three levels. Choosing only to use the middle or comprehensive level, however, assumes that the contributions of those results will be responsive to societal requirements and realities. In actual practice, any organization operates in all three levels whether or not they formally realize that fact, or formally plan to integrate and relate them. Choosing the strategic (holistic) level for a needs assessment will better assure the integration of all levels.

(3) Identify the Needs Assessment and Planning Partners

Successful needs assessment depends upon finding the correct partners to both guide the process and "own" it when it is completed and applied (Drucker, 1973). An otherwise good plan may fail simply because uninvolved or unrepresented people may not understand that an imposed change (no matter how rational) might benefit them. The adoption of any plan and resulting changes is usually helped by having the people affected act as partners (or at least be represented) in its creation.

THE PLANNING PARTNERS

There are three human needs assessment and planning partner groups, and one performance data-based one. The partners include those: (a) who will be affected by or be the recipients of any intervention, (b) who will implement the plan, and (c) citizens, such as employers and neighbors (and/or society) which receive the outputs. In an educational organization, these partners would be all or realistic representatives of learners, educators, and society/community. (Another "partner," but a non-human one, is contributed by the "hard" data, comprising observed actual performance and results.)

The exact group members to serve on the planning team depend upon the nature of the specific educational agency. Usually the educational planners, perhaps the school district's planning director, or superintendent in a small district, will be the ones to get the needs assessment into motion. Other members of the professional education staff will serve as the "implementer's" partner group. The recipients may be the immediate clients of the planners (e.g., students, special education learners, adults, senior citizens, emotion-

Society / Community

Figure 3.1. The three human representative educational planning partners include educators, learners, and community/society members.

ally disturbed, etc.). "Society" includes those who will be affected by what a school system is able to deliver (e.g., to employers, community members, etc.).

When selecting the planning partners, assure that they are representative of their actual constituencies. If ethnic composition is important, assure a proportional sample; if age is an important variable, include appropriate groups; if particular skills and competencies are critical, assure that these are represented among the partners; if particular educational levels (e.g., elementary, middle, high school) are important, include them in the partnership. Usually, a stratified random sample of each partner group will assure proper representation.

Don't make the planning team a huge group—just representative. Big numbers are not necessarily useful, usually only difficult to work with. The exact number of planning partners depends upon what is being planned, and whom the planned changes are supposed to serve. The partner groups should represent the actual world of learners, educators, and community and thus should not include "tokens" nor be packed with friends.

THE NEEDS DATA

The word "need" has several possible meanings. The one used here defines "need" only as a gap in results, not a gap in resources or processes. The term "quasi-need" describes a gap in processes, how-to-do-its, inputs, or resources such as level of education, budget, time of students in class, teacher training, available equipment, support personnel, rules and regulations, laws, and wishes of important people.

When defining needs, write the statements the same way you would a measurable objective (cf. Mager, 1975). Each "need statement" will, without confusion, specify what performance is expected, who or what will display that performance, under what conditions the performance will be observed, and what criteria will be used to measure success. Because a need statement is bipolar— stating "what is" and "what should be"—each "pole" of the need statement will be written according to the specifications for a measurable objective. (It is understood that the "what is" statement is not, strictly speaking, an objective since it describes a current state of affairs. However, the characteristics of a measurable objective may still be applicable, although shifted to the present tense.)

The representative educational planning partners will supply judgments, or "perceived" needs. Because these are based upon personal experiences and feelings, this source is termed needs-sensing data. Sensed needs provide both perceived reality and sensitivity to issues of values and preferences about current problems and consequences. In addition, they may reveal observations concerning the methods and procedures used in getting the currently undesired or inadequate results. This type of data is often called "soft" because of its attitudinal and perspective origins. Most so-called needs assessments and need analyses discussed in the literature are actually needs-sensing approaches alone.

When harvesting needs data, an additional reality is critical: hard data-based needs ("hard" because derived from actual controlled, independently verifiable, observed performance and consequences). Hard data are concerned with actual human and educational gaps in performance. Hard data might include societal consequences (outcomes) such as organizational image, death rates, numbers of people with positive credit ratings, quality of community life, etc. Other hard data might include "internal" educational performance gaps associated with indicators such as productivity, failures, truancy, graffiti, counseling case completions, absenteeism, morale, complaints, or outputs such as number of job placements and, acceptances and completion of post-secondary education.

These additional controlled observations, data-based performance referents act as a "non-human partner"; they supply additional reality to be considered in identifying, documenting, and selecting needs.

Together, the sensed needs from the human partners plus the performance-based data will serve as the "partners for planning" (Figure 3.2).

The combination of sensed needs from the human partners and the "hard" data from controlled observations of performance will provide the solid evidence required to decide on practical programs, projects, interventions, and changes (Figure 3.3).

Society / Community

Performance Data of Educational Results
and Societal Impact Consequences

Figure 3.2. The planning partners for needs assessment include three human partners (implementers, recipients, and society/community) plus the data-based performance data.

INDICATORS OF SOCIETAL IMPACT AND CONSEQUENCES

In spite of some "conventional wisdom" to the contrary, there are
indicators (imprecise, but useful agreed-upon calibrations) of societal
impact (cf. Kaufman, Corrigan and Johnson, 1969; Kaufman and
Carron, 1980) in terms of learner self-sufficiency upon completion or
termination of schooling. One <u>minimal</u> specification of expected
educational outcome is:

> by the time the learner legally exits the educational agency, s/he
> will be at, and continue to be at, a self-sufficiency point or beyond
> (modified from Kaufman, 1972).

Self-sufficiency, a point where an individual's consumption is equal
to or less than one's production, may be measured with another
<u>indicator</u>: money. Production is anything one gets paid for, consump-
tion is something for which monies are expended (Figure 3.4).

While it is not altogether comforting to view the indicator of self-
sufficiency in terms of money, it is generally true that people put
money where their values lie. (People often spend more on alcohol
than they do on educational improvement, more on drugs than they
do on preschool education, more on politician's wages than on beginning teachers' salaries.)

Put another way, if educational agencies are not intending to
assist learners to be self-sufficient, self-reliant, and fully functioning
human beings, then exactly what are their intentions? Education
should be humanistic enough to be accountable for contributing to
individual learner success and functioning in today's and tomorrow's
worlds. Can we afford anything less?

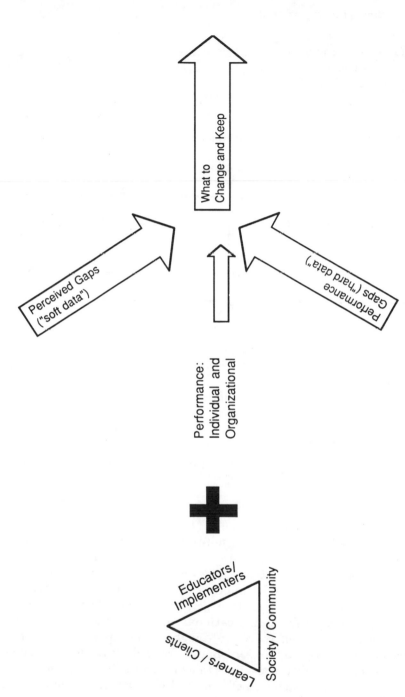

Figure 3.3 Needs assessments are a partnership approach which combines both perceptions ("soft" data) and actual performance ("hard" data) in determining what to keep and what to change.

SYMBOLS: > Greater than
           = Equal to
           < Less than

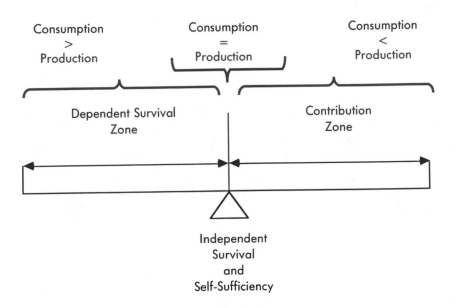

A continuum of individual utility in our society. After Kaufman, 1972.

Figure 3.4. Self-sufficiency may be indicated by the point where one's consumption is equal to or less than that which is produced.

ADDING CONCERN FOR QUALITY OF LIFE

To be sure, self-sufficiency and self-reliance are critical and must be included as a basic variable in needs assessment and the planning of any educational system. Once survival has been achieved or assured, it is time to consider making "life worth living." Quality of life includes such factors as love, joy, art, music, drama, dance, friendships, relationships. Educational planning should include these in any sensible effort. While "tough-minded" planning is certain to look at money and time, it should also include the formal consideration of the quality of the lives to which education is responsive and responsible. The inclusion of two addition variables when using the OEM "template" for system planning is strongly urged:

SELF-SUFFICIENCY
FACTORS

QUALITY OF LIFE
FACTORS

When planning an educational system, concern for achieving both self-sufficiency as well as a positive quality of life should be formally included in the process and criteria. First, place our primary focus upon the essentials of "staying alive," and when this is in-place or assured, then plan to assist people to have a satisfying, productive, and enjoyable life.

HUMAN CONCERN IS VITAL AND INCLUDED

While not readily apparent in this model, there are some very human concerns "hidden" but part of this formulation. For example, positive mental health contributes to a person not being below the independent survival point. Happiness and self-confidence and positive self-esteem are components in one's being productive. If an individual is greatly depressed, does not get along with others, is estranged from loved ones, or has a debilitating anxiety, she or he may not be able to function well enough to be self-sufficient (cf. the literature on "humanistic" approaches to human behavior, including Frankl, 1962; Laswell, 1948; Rogers, 1964). In fact, it is hypothesized that happy people (cf. Greenwald and Rich, 1984) will be more likely to be at or beyond the self-sufficiency point. Positive quality of life is a very important consideration in planning.

*(4) Obtain the Needs Assessment and Planning
Partners' Participation*

It is not enough to identify the partners; they also must become willing, active contributors to the planning process and products. When contacting the partners tell each of the expectations, time commitments, desired products, and required contributions. Reveal the extent to which they will be supported (funds, travel, release time, data, materials, available support services, etc.) and the extent to which their products will really be considered and used. Obtain their commitment, schedule them, and design the first meeting (which can be face-to-face or through surveys, perception/opinion gathering techniques, teleconferencing, or computer interface). If they don't attend and/or don't contribute, replace them with those who will.

(5) Obtain Planning Partners' Acceptance of the Needs Assessment and Planning Level to be Used

In step two (above), three levels were suggested: middle, comprehensive, and holistic. Share the characteristics of each of the possible levels with the partners, and get their commitment to one. By letting them know the array of alternative frameworks along with the advantages and disadvantages of each—the questions each will pose and answer—their choice will be informed, and they will know what they will be doing and missing (if they do not choose the holistic option). It is important that the scope of the needs assessment be known and agreed upon by all partners, and that there will be a common set of understandings and expectations.

Explain to the partners the basic concepts of needs assessment: the process for identifying, documenting, and justifying the gaps between What Is and What Should Be for results—products, outputs (both internal to the organization), and/or outcomes (external consequences)—and placing the gaps (needs) in priority order for closure (see Figure 3.5). There may be three kinds of needs assessments, one relating to gaps between What Is and What Should Be for each of the three types of results (products, outputs, and outcomes).

(6) Collect Needs Data (Both Internal and External)

Depending upon the needs assessment level the partners have selected, collect external and/or internal data. Internal needs data concern performance discrepancies within your educational system or school, and external needs data concern performance discrepancies of your students and completers (and graduates) while functioning in their (and your) world.

Gaps in results between "what is" and "what should be" may be collected for each item in the results chain:

WHAT IS	WHAT SHOULD BE
Societal Goals/Requirements ⟷	Societal Goals/Requirements
System Goals/Requirements ⟷	System Goals/Requirements
Individual School Goals/ ⟷	Individual School Goals/
Requirements	Requirements
Subject "N" Goal/Requirements ⟷	Subject "N" Goal/ Requirements
Supervisor B Objectives ⟷	Supervisor B Objectives
Teacher B Objectives ⟷	Teacher B Objectives
Learner B Objectives ⟷	Learner B Objectives
Learner Products ⟷	Learner Products
Activities/Interventions ⟷	Activities/Interventions
Resources/Inputs ⟷	Resources/Inputs

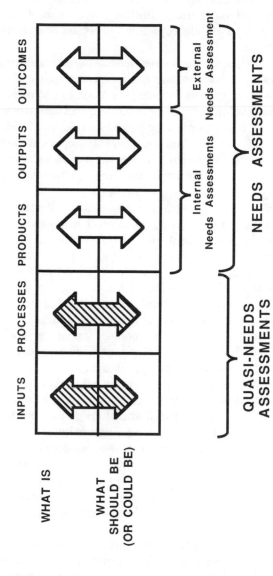

Figure 3.5. Relating external and internal needs assessments on the basis of the five organizational elements. The open arrows show possible needs assessments, and the cross-hatched arrows are possible quasi-needs assessments. (Based in part upon Kaufman, R., "Planning and Organizational Improvement Terms," Oct. 1983. Reprinted by permission of *Performance and Instruction.*)

There is a surprising amount of data available from public sources: departments of employment, labor, health, police, and census. When collecting data on internal performance, two sources should be accessed: (a) the perceptions of the planning partners, and (b) the actual performance and payoff discrepancies collected from controlled, objective observations.

The collection of perceptions—needs-sensing—concerning performance discrepancies may be accomplished through a variety of tools and methods ranging from face-to-face meetings to remote data collection methods including rating scales, questionnaires, structured interviews, or other paper-and-pencil assessments. Many response collecting instruments, methods, and strategies are available (cf. Witkin, 1984). The "sensed needs" of the partners will supply data concerning those performance discrepancies which they feel are important. People's perceptions are their realities.

In designing or selecting needs-sensing data collection instruments it is important that they pose the correct unbiased questions. Make certain that the instrument and its questions are focusing responses on results, not on resources (inputs) or methods and techniques (processes). Also, make the questions broad-based enough to cover the possible array of needs without burdening the respondents with overly complex issues and time-consuming length. Make it easy for them to respond. The data collection instruments (be they structured interviews or written responses) must be both valid (measuring that which they are really supposed to measure) and reliable (measuring the same thing consistently).

Obtaining internal educational performance data is usually easier than it first appears. Most organizations have a lot of hard data; one only has to figure out what is wanted and then go looking for it, for example, student grades, teacher ratings, detentions, extracurricular activities and accomplishments, tardiness, absenteeism, production rates, counseling cases closed, audit exceptions, courses completed, certified competencies, sick leave, work samples, retention rates, etc. Look for validity and reliability of these data, and use them only when they will supply useful information concerning performance.

When collecting outside-of-the-organization performance data—if the holistic framework has been selected—one frequently finds useful information both within and external to the organization (for example, data concerning citizens' perceptions and satisfaction, employer evaluations, delinquency, funding levels, complaints, arrests, income, credit ratings, etc.).

SELF-SUFFICIENCY DATA ARE AVAILABLE

Many existing public agencies have or can get access to data relative to the economic level and societal status of in-school and former learners. For example, human services agencies often have records of people on government transfer payments (e.g., welfare, relief, food stamps, aid to dependent children), employment, taxes paid, and military service. This information might be accessed by name or social security number if the privacy of each individual is strictly maintained. Thus, if this type of data is to be used, it must be for groups of people, not for individuals, in order to protect their rights and privacy. Laws and regulations about access to such data vary, and must be carefully respected. Additional indirect sources include indicators of self-sufficiency and good citizenship such as from questionnaires, use of vocational education placement-and-follow-up results, interviews, and review and analysis of published public records which are often reported by census tracts.

Depending upon the selected level for the needs assessment (middle, comprehensive, or holistic) different data (and thus tools with which to collect it) are useful. In general, the following guidance (Kaufman, 1986a) is offered:

Type of Needs Assessment (Level)	Primary Concern	Tool(s) or Data to be Considered
middle	gaps in student &/or teacher accomplishments.	job task analysis testing, etc.
comprehensive	gaps in school accomplishments (plus middle-level)	combined test results student records institutional audits # of graduates # of dropouts, etc.
holistic/strategic	societal contributions (plus middle and comprehensive levels)	demographics public agency records federal records placement and follow-up data questionnaires interviews, etc.

Both hard and soft data should be used, and should focus upon results, not on methods, means, processes, techniques, procedures, resources, money, time, or personnel. The targeting of results in needs assessment is essential in order to relate means and ends.

(7) List Identified and Documented Needs

Before setting priorities, deriving objectives and selecting interventions, it is necessary to obtain a set of agreed upon needs. The needs identified by each partner group may be recorded in a needs matrix (cf. Kaufman and English, 1979) which lists needs for each of the partner groups such as shown in Figure 3.6.

It is likely that each partner group will generate several different subsequent versions of their matrix as they discuss the nature of their perceptions and experiences, and continue to shift from their more familiar process (or solution) orientation to a results orientation (Kaufman and English, 1979). It is important to encourage a results-only orientation. If solutions keep reappearing, list them and note that these will be considered as possible tactics and approaches during the methods-means analysis phase when solutions are selected to meet the identified needs.

GETTING AGREEMENT

Sometimes the partners will not agree on the needs to be included on the list. However, substantial agreement will have to be obtained before moving ahead. Some possible methods for obtaining agreement include:

- Translate the disputed perceived needs (which are often not needs stated as gaps in results but are gaps in resources or processes) into results and ask the partners if the revision represents their concern. If it does, list them. If it does not, ask them to revise it into a results statement which will. Most arguments over "needs" are really over gaps in methods and resources (quasi-needs), not actual gaps in results.
- Ask the disagreeing partners to define the "result which will be obtained if this 'need' were to be met." This encourages the partners to track the linkages from processes to results, and then to a defined gap in results. Then, these needs can be included in the ranking.
- Discourage special interest groups from "pushing" a solution (such as computer-aided instruction, time management training), a method (self-paced instruction, multi-media), or a re-

	WHAT IS	WHAT SHOULD BE
LEARNERS/ CLIENTS	30% of graduates are unemployed as reported by 1989 Department of Employment (DOE) report X-11; Follow-up studies by Dept. of Employment (report X-11a, 1991) show 55% of the graduates are below poverty level. 45% of graduates are in college, and of these 17% are in the contribution area as measured by their income. 58% of the graduates are white, and 56% of the total graduation group are below the national reading norms as measured by the Fenwick Test of Reading achievement (DOE Rpt. X-11a), and 66% are below norms on math as measured by the Naples test of Mathematic Competency (DOE Rpt. X-11a). In the sample, 95% of past graduates want higher income, and 11% have served or are serving jail sentences (DOE Rpt. X-11a). Etc.	100% of graduates should be at or beyond the self-sufficiency point, as reported by an independent audit of income "in" and expenses "out" for a stratified random sample of those legally exiting from the school system, and certified correct by the associate superintendent for instruction. There shall be no graduates of those legally exiting who have been arrested and convicted of any crime above a $100 fine for a period of five years as measured by the certification of the associate superintendent for instruction. There will be no significant difference (.05 level of confidence or beyond) in self sufficiency and contribution of those legally exiting within five years of exit, on the basis of color, race, creed, sex, age, religion, or national origin as certified by an independent audit of a stratified random sample and certified correct by the associate superintendent for instruction. Etc.
EDUCATORS/ IMPLEMEN-TERS	97% of teachers in the district are credentialed as certified by the State Department of Teacher Licensing (1988). 78% of them feel that minorities can perform as well as majority learners (District Study 87-2, April 1987). 55% of teachers demonstrated competencies for math and reading required by the state performance criteria during the last teacher certifi-cation renewal period (Dept. of Education Report 1010, June 1988); 83% of teachers and educators are whites, and 76% have 5 or more years certifiable experience (Dept. of Ed. Report 1010, June 1989). Etc.	75% feel that only 50% of the learners can reach independent survival or beyond within five years of legal exit, as reported by a survey conducted by the school district (District Study 87-2), and the same study indicates that 80% of the teachers feel that only 10% of the learners can reach the contribution zone. In the same study, it was found that 91% of the educators felt that at least double the monies now spent on education is required to have any more measurable success, and 94% felt that teaching loads must be decreased at least 50% for any change to occur. Etc.
SOCIETY/ COMMUNITY	90% of stratified random sample of community members feel that too much money is spent on education, and 88% feel that the teachers are only responsible for making learners get and keep jobs after high school completion (as reported in District study 78-2, April 1990). Etc.	100% of learners should get and keep jobs after they leave public schools (as reported by District Study 88-2) and 88% felt (reported by the same study) that no more public funds should be spent for public education. Etc.

Figure 3.6. A needs matrix displays the needs identified for each partner group. (Based in part upon Kaufman and English, 1979, *Needs Assessment: Concept and Application.* Used with permission, Educational Technology Publications.)

source (money, people) without first identifying and selecting the need to which their favorite solution is intended to be responsive.

- Encourage (even insist) all partners to define needs as gaps in results. Get everyone to do the same for themselves and other partners.

For example, some planning partners might have operational difficulties with confusing means and ends, and still will push for the acceptance of a process gap (or quasi-need) such as:

> "We 'need' computers to teach computer literacy for tomorrow's high-tech world." The problem with this statement, regardless of how well meaning, is that it refers to a means, not an end, nor a gap in results.
>
> Ask "if we used computers, what would the impact, or results be, and how would we know?"
>
> They might give a first answer of "then the learners would know about computers, and then they won't be scared of something which will be part of their future."
>
> By redefining their concerns into an end, or result, you might recode their wish into a statement of results, and then ask "If we did do that, how would it be if we stated that as 'each learner will be able to write at least a basic computer program which will correctly solve a mathematical problem. In addition, each one will score at the mid-point or beyond on the validated Byte Test of Computer Literacy and Comfort before they graduate or complete high school.' " If they agree, then the planning team could collect "what is" data for the students and determine if there is a what is/what should be gap in performance and attitude . . . a need.

- Be patient, open, listen. Others bring experience and expertise to the planning team; nobody has "a corner on wisdom."

Based upon the previous steps and the resulting data, an actual list of the gaps in results is derived and provided to all of the partners. It is frequently useful to place the identified needs in a "needs assessment summary table" (Kaufman, 1972; Kaufman and English, 1979) such as in Figure 3.7.

(8) Place Needs in Priority Order and Reconcile Disagreements

One useful approach to prioritization is to provide each of the three partner groups with the list of needs based upon soft data plus the hard data from actual performance and then ask each to:

(a) Reconcile the sensed-needs with those based upon the hard data.

	WHAT IS (OUTCOMES)	WHAT SHOULD BE (OUTCOMES)
LEARNERS/ CLIENTS	30% of graduates are currently unemployed. 55% of graduates are below poverty level. 45% of graduates are in college. 17% of graduates are in the contribution area. 48% of graduates are female. 58% of graduates are white. 56% of graduates were below norms on 11th grade math test. 95% of graduates want more income. 1% of graduates now have jail record. Etc.	100% of learners currently in the system and all graduates and those legally exiting want to be at the self-sufficiency point or beyond as measured by their consumption at least equalling their production; no bankruptcy for any graduate or person legally exiting, no commitments to mental institutions, no person arrested and found guilty of a felony, or misdemeanor which is punishable by a fine greater than $250.00, a divorce rate which is significantly lower than the national divorce rate; all of the above measured by a stratified random sample certified as correct by a licensed psychometrician. There will be no significant difference between those legally exiting from the educational system on the above indicators which are attributable to color, race, creed, sex, age, religion, or national origin at or beyond the .05 level of confidence, as certified by a licensed psychometrician. Etc.
EDUCATORS/ IMPLEMEN- TERS	97% of teachers are creden- tialed by the state for the sub- jects taught. 55% demonstrate the minimal competency re- quired for certification of new teachers in the teaching areas. 83% of the teachers are white. 76% of the teachers have 5 or more years of teaching experi- ence. Etc.	Same as above plus: 100% of the teachers will have the minimal competencies required for certification of new teachers in the teaching areas which were based upon a needs assessment conducted which identified and operationally defined the skills, knowledges, and attitudes required of learners to be self- sufficient and contribute in the next twenty years, as measured by state validated criterion- referenced test of achievement in the competency areas, as reported by State certifi- cation reports for all teachers in the system. If additional resources are required, the school board will vote to make them available, and justification will be supplied by the teachers and justified on a "value-added" basis where the additional resources will demonstrate a positive return-on-investment relative to all other possible alternatives and the considera- tions of no acquisition of new resources. Etc.
SOCIETY/ COMMUNITY	90% feel that too much money is currently being spent on education. 88% feel that only the teachers are responsible for making learners get and keep jobs upon exit from the schools. Etc.	Same as "what should be" for learners above plus: additional expenditures will be approved by a majority of the school board, and will not require any additional bond election or tax override revenues for the next five years. Etc.

Figure 3.7 A further-developed needs matrix (based upon Figure 3.6) which has been improved and tightened through group action. (Based in part upon Kaufman and English, 1979, *Needs Assessment: Concept and Application.* Used with permission, Educational Technology Publications.)

(b) Derive a common set of needs which are supported by both the hard and soft data (and request additional data if there are insurmountable differences; see step nine below).

(c) Set priorities among the needs.

In order to set priorities, criteria for weighting them should be selected. One useful approach is asking the partners to assign a value (often in monetary terms) for each need in terms of:

- What will it cost to reduce or eliminate the need?
- What will it cost to ignore the need?

"Cost" may be seen in financial as well as in quality of life terms. A number of useful and more complex criteria are available (cf. Witkin, 1984; Kaufman and Stone, 1983).

Then each partner group may meet with one of the others and derive a common set of rankings. This combined group then meets with the remaining group and together defines a final, all-inclusive set of rankings of the needs.

INCLUDING THE PAST AND THE FUTURE

History and the future are other variables to be considered in a needs assessment. Time is useful in order to shape the future, for it provides us with the potential to manage forthcoming events (cf. Drucker, 1985). Responding to contemporary problems requires us to react and also (if we allow it) provides us with the opportunity to design and deliver a more useful future.

History provides a context in which to evaluate the past and make some predictions about the future (Stakenas and Mock, 1985). The study and formal consideration of possible alternative future consequences provide optional payoffs and quality of life possibilities from which to choose alternative tomorrows. Needs assessment and planning are useful to the extent to which we define and move towards a more productive and satisfying future.

While this book does not provide extensive sources and methods for identifying and using indicators of future conditions, possibilities, and opportunities, the literature is quite rich and extensive (cf. Myers, 1984; Phi Delta Kappa, 1984; issues of *The Futurist* published by the World Futures Society). Sociological, psychological, and economic studies, to name a few disciplines studying the future, provide trends, directions, demographics, and data concerning where our world is going, what is likely to occur if nothing is done to intervene, and what possibilities exist among which the needs assessment and planning partners may choose.

Demographic studies and data provide an invaluable window into the future. By identifying changes, trends, and issues which will impact our schools and society, planners cannot only identify and calibrate "what will be" but also start a dialogue to better determine "what could be" and "what should be." Studies of and concern for demographics (cf. Hodgkinson, 1985; 1986; Myers, 1984) are increasing and deserve the serious attention of any planning effort.

A basic set of criteria by which gaps between current and future societal possibilities may be initiated using the self-sufficiency criteria noted earlier in this chapter should include: what is the current level of self-sufficiency and self-reliance, what will it be like in the future if everything "drifts" into the future, and what could a better world be like?

Sometimes there are differences of opinion which stall everything. Don't go ahead without substantial agreement, and don't cave in to "keep peace." Most partners really do want to get the right needs identified and met. Often what is missing are appropriate additional data.

Frequently, the hard and soft data "disagree," causing a mismatch. Usually additional (and more responsive) data should be obtained. Build a matrix comparing the perceived needs and the hard data-based needs. When there is a mismatch, collect more data using a revision of the techniques selected in Step 6. When agreement is reached, the needs assessment and planning process may move ahead.

By "merging" both opinion and performance-based results data, a needs assessor/planner may find areas where there is common agreement on needs; and where there is not consensus, initiate either further fact-finding or education of the partners to achieve agreement.

A flow process for merging the two types of data and deciding the areas for collecting additional information is shown in Figure 3.8.

Basic agreement should exist between the hard and soft data to assure that the needs assessment results will be perceived as useful and will be accepted by the partners and those they represent.

When disagreement still lingers, it is often useful to review the historical context and the futures data to provide a frame of reference concerning "what was," "what is," "what will be," "what could be," and finally selecting "what should be."

(9) List Problems (Selected Needs) to be Resolved and Obtain Agreement of Partners

A problem is a need selected for resolution. No gap in results, no need; no need, no problem. Problems considered for resolution may

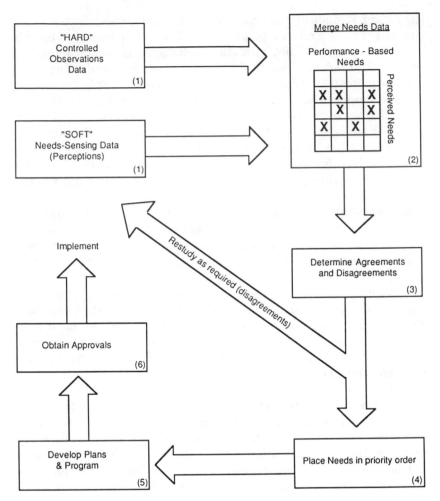

Figure 3.8. Merging "hard" and "soft" data in a needs assessment in order to set priorities and select useful interventions.

be either a list, or in the form of a needs assessment summary matrix of the variety shown in Figure 3.7.

RELATING NEEDS TO RESOURCES

The array of needs may later (during a methods-means analysis) be compared to a projected budget (either requested or allocated); the priorities are used to assign funds until the total sum is exhausted. Sometimes additional budget may be justified by asking decision makers to reconsider the previous budget allocation based upon the solid needs assessment data and the partnership-derived priorities.

After the problems have been selected, and budgets obtained, but before work begins, make certain that the partners agree with the final results. If they do not, have them recommend modifications and derive the justification for revisions to the decision makers.

using the needs data

A needs assessment provides the direction and criteria for system planning and accomplishment. By identifying needs and providing criteria for selecting where the system should be heading, the mission for an educational system may be specified.

Needs, when prioritized and selected for resolution, provide problems. "Problems" identify the selected gaps between current results and desired ones which serve as the basis for planning to get from "what is" to "what should be."

The balance of this book is about using the needs in defining mission objectives, and identifying what must be accomplished to achieve educational success: meet the needs. The tools and techniques of system analysis will identify what results have to be accomplished (and in what order) to meet the needs.

needs assessments are practical

A results-oriented needs assessment, such as one described using these ten steps, provides a basis for identifying, defining, justifying, and selecting needs. From the partner-derived needs, problems may be stated, selected, and defined as gaps in results to be closed. These in turn will provide the criteria for precise objectives which serve as the practical basis for further planning and the identification and selection of methods and means to meet the needs and resolve the problems (Kaufman and Thiagarajan, 1987).

The model suggested here is not a kit or package which may be taken out of a box and used. It will require the user to employ it as a guide to mesh with individual agency characteristics and requirements. Many models and techniques abound (cf. Witkin, 1984) and alternatives should be considered. The choice of actual models and techniques should be made, however, on the basis of what a needs assessment has to deliver for functional planning to take place, not simply on the ease of doing one.

Conducting a needs assessment does not have to be expensive nor time-consuming. Outcome data are available, as are many forms of output and product data. Needs-sensing data may be collected by using or modifying a number of available instruments, or instruments that can be constructed.

Deriving and using needs assessment and planning partner groups may superficially seem time-consuming (and a bit bothersome). Modern partnership groups represent a growing trend toward involving significant people in organizational decisions and activities (cf. Peters and Waterman, 1982; Peters and Austin, 1985; Kanter, 1983; Kaufman and Stone, 1983).

Using needs assessment provides a cost-useful alternative to designing educational interventions which disappoint . . . while they do meet product level objectives they fail to contribute to the organization's value to the students, the communities which pay the bills of education, professional staff, and school system employees. It is less expensive to find out where an educational system should be headed, why it should go there, and then tailor interventions to accomplish this than it is to fail and have to search out what went wrong, why it failed, and try again.

glossary

Hard data   independently verifiable data which have been derived from controlled observations of performance, status, condition, or actual consequences.

Needs matrix   a table showing "What is" and "What should be" for each of the planning partner groups of learners, educators, and society/community.

Needs sensing   the collection of the perceptions, values, desires, and experiences of one or more individuals. Many so-called needs assessments, especially those using questionnaires and interview methods, are really needs-sensing activities.

Quality of life factors   important variables which characterize a "life worth living" including satisfaction with one's situation, environment, activities, and relationships.

Self-sufficiency   the state where an individual is not under the care, custody, or control of another person, agency, or substance. One indicator of self-sufficiency is when an individual's consumption is equal to or less than his or her production.

Soft data   data based upon the perceptions, values, desires, and experiences of one or more individuals. They are judgmental in nature.

Summary needs assessment matrix   the summarizing needs matrix which displays the selected needs as gaps between "what is" and "what should be" for results of the needs assessment and planning partners.

Want   a method, means, technique, process, or solution which one prefers.

exercises

1. What are the three types of needs assessments? What are the advantages and disadvantages of each?

2. What are the differences between "needs" and "quasi-needs"?

3. Why is it important that a needs assessment deal with ends, not means?

4. What are the differences between "needs" and "wants"?

5. What is wrong with the following need statement: "Increase the school day and the school year to achieve 'excellence'"? Modify it so that it is a useful need statement.

6. What are the possible criteria for prioritizing needs?

7. List the nine suggested steps for doing a needs assessment.

8. What is the role of values in conducting a needs assessment?

9. Identify five documented needs for your school system. Write them in appropriate form for a needs assessment summary table.

10. What is the relationship between needs assessment and problem solving?

11. Why is it important to formally consider both self-sufficiency and quality of life factors in educational planning?

12. What is the role and importance of the future in deriving a useful educational plan?

CHAPTER 4
mission analysis

EDUCATIONAL PLANNING (USING a system approach) consists of identifying and justifying problems and then identifying what must be accomplished to resolve them. Identifying and justifying problems is the major concern of needs assessment. Defining what must be accomplished is a role of problem solving. Useful in problem solving is system analysis: identifying what must be accomplished in order to meet the identified needs.

The major purpose of a system analysis is to identify the requirements for problem solving and further discover possible ways to accomplish each requirement. From an identified and selected problem based on documented needs, one should resolve the problem by identifying all of its characteristics, determine interrelations among the parts of the problem, and specify measurable requirements for reaching the best solution to the problem and each of its parts.

Frequently, educational problems are presented in relatively global and diffuse terms. However, an educational planner or designer is required to determine the exact nature of the problem so that a precise referent is available against which further analysis, design, implementation, and evaluation may take place. For instance, an educational mission (overall intent) of "developing each child to her/his own capacity" provides little usable information to a planner. What is necessary is a more precise goal statement covering the actual range of capacities and the entry characteristics of the learners. Identifying the actual skills, knowledge, attitudes, and abilities required for successful completion of the mission is also necessary.

Specification of exactly what is to be delivered as a result of planned activity is usually a gritty, grinding experience the first few times it is undertaken. However, as with any other learned behavior, the skills improve, and each time system analysis is applied to educational planning, less time and effort are required. (Remember the first time you slipped behind the wheel of a car to learn how to drive, confronting an array of knobs, levers, and pedals? Surely this was a skill far too complex for you to master. In retrospect, driving was fairly simple to learn, and for the most part we now drive almost automatically.) With practice, the skills required in system analysis will become easier and easier to use, and the results from valid educational planning should be well worth the effort.

The educational problem-solving effort is most efficient and effective when legitimate high-priority problems are identified, selected, and analyzed, and are based on documented needs as described in the previous chapter. Recall from the first three chapters the relationship between needs and problems. An educational need, as we define it here, is a measurable gap between our current outcomes (or outputs or products) and our desired (or required) ones. When we perform a needs assessment, we end up with a number of gaps which are placed in priroity order, and the gaps to be eliminated are stated. The gaps, once selected for closure are the problems. Thus, problems are selected gaps in results (needs). If we have no gaps, then we have no problems.

The needs selected for resolution provide the starting point for system analysis in general and mission analysis in particular.

what is a mission?

A mission is an overall job—an outcome, output, or product; a completed service; or a change in the condition of something or somebody—that must be accomplished. Mission analysis is a determination of "where we are going," "how we know when we have arrived," and "what the major steps are to get from here to there." Since educational planning should consistently build on acquired analytical data, the planner must be sure that the data being used are as complete, correct, and current as possible. A valid and precise base for making this first and crucial results-to-be-delivered commitment is imperative.

Mission Analysis Elements

As defined here, mission analysis consists of two parts:
- mission objective and associated performance requirements
- mission profile

Both of these elements are described, along with the process by which they are derived.

the mission objective

A mission objective is a precise statement expressed in perfor-mance terms which specifies the results of a mission. The mission objective may be derived from a goal relative to meeting a need. The purpose of framing a mission objective is to translate such an intent into the measurable, most general—yet inclusive—statement of the required result (mission) that can be made. Examples of poorly stated "missions" for an educational planner could include:

- Build a high school.
- Determine learner needs in the Chase-Kane School District.
- Hire new teachers.
- Develop an instructional computing center.

Although many problems are given to us in these terms, such man-dates do not contain enough information to allow planners to go to work. We have to be more explicit if we are to proceed with con-fidence that our effort will be efficient, effective, and useful.

Mission objectives are performance objectives that specify results (ideally outcomes) in measurable terms. Because a holistic frame of reference is recommended, you are encouraged to identify any mis-sion as relating to an outcome. It should be remembered, however, that the other units of analysis are legitimate, and thus a mission objective may relate to products, outputs or outcomes.

Any mission objective requires the same degree of specificity as any other performance or behavioral objectives, such as those described by Mager (1975). Therefore, a mission objective must state precisely the following conditions for any desired or required result:

(1) What performance or result is to be demonstrated?

(2) Who or what will display the performance or result?

(3) Under what conditions is the result or performance to be demonstrated?

(4) What specific criteria will be used to determine if the perfor-mance or result has been achieved?

In addition, a fifth condition should be met:

(5) There will be no misunderstandings concerning what is to be accomplished.

[A brief warning about preparing objectives: Many educators are pragmatic people. They are used to swinging into action, and getting things going. It is tempting for such action-oriented people to include how a result or performance will be brought about (methods, means, tactics, how-to-do-its), and thus lock themselves into a solution before defining the problem. A hallmark of a system approach is the specification of gaps in results (ends) before selecting the how-to-do-its (means). Therefore, any objective should not have the methods and means for getting the results included in the statement. The determination of how to reach the objective will be made after a methods-means analysis (Chapter 6) has been completed.]

Mission objectives, one variety of objectives which share the five characteristics listed above, designate exactly where one is going and/or what is to be produced. Look at the following hypothetical mission objectives:

Unacceptable—Design a biology curriculum. (This is a statement of general intent, not a mission objective.)

Better—By June 30, three years from now, at least 90 percent of biology learners with XYZ characteristics in the Chase-Kane School District will achieve Z performance on L criterion measure. (This objective is more specific and precise than its predecessor. It states precisely what is going to be accomplished, under what conditions, and to what degree; therefore, it better meets the requirements for a mission objective. It is a product-level mission objective.)

In performing a mission analysis we start by specifying what has to be accomplished: the statement of the mission, sometimes in general terms only, is the first step.[9] Some examples of general starting points might be:

(1) Get and retrieve an astronaut on Mars, unharmed, within ten years, within budget.

(2) Reduce fatal traffic accidents in California by 15 percent next year.

(3) Eliminate illiteracy in Janice County within five years.

A more complete example would be:

(4) Increase by 17 percent per year each year for the next five years the number of completers of the Jac School District who are

---

[9]When using a holistic system approach, the needs assessment data will directly provide the mission objective and performance requirements in the "what should be" statement.

self-sufficient and self-reliant as indicated by positive credit
ratings and no arrests, unemployment, divorces, or welfare receipt.
The accomplishment of this will be certified by the Superintendent of Schools on the first school day of each new calendar year.

Notice that each of the foregoing statements has both quantitative
and qualitative aspects. Let us break down the first illustration:

What is to be accomplished?	Get to Mars.
Who or what will display it?	An astronaut.
Under what condition?	By ten years from now, with a budget of $X.
What criteria (how much or how well) will be used?	Return trip, 100 percent, and unharmed.

Now, let's break down the mission components of our fourth
example:

What is to be accomplished?	A 17 percent per year increase in self-sufficiency
Who or what will display it?	Completers of the Jac School District
Under what condition?	Each year for five years
What criteria (how much or how well) will be used?	Positive credit, no divorces, no unemployment, arrests, or welfare recipients. Certified around January 2 of each school year by the Superintendent.

In order to assure communication, the terms and performance criteria used in a mission objective must be understood by all who will
deal with that objective and its accomplishment. There should be no
confusion concerning the results to be accomplished among the
educational partners.

Because of the results-orientation and the required precision, a
mission objective must also include the basis for evaluation. Since
loose or nebulous terms such as appreciate and feel are not meaningful unless they are defined operationally, every effort must be
made to eliminate areas of misconception or misinterpretation.

An important characteristic of a mission objective, which is more
relevant to curriculum objectives than to managerial and administrative ones, is the requirement to "focus on the learner" and his/her
ultimate ability to be a contributing, successful member of today's
and tomorrow's societies.

There are, then, four conditions stated in a useful mission objective and together they must show at least three characteristics:

Conditions	Characteristics
1. What is to be displayed in order to demonstrate completion?	Objectives must communicate successfully to all users and evaluators. All of the conditions for measuring results must be specified and must contain the basis for evaluation; they must be in measurable performance terms which are valid and leave no room for confusion.
2. Who or what is to demonstrate completion?	
3. Under what conditions is it to be demonstrated?	
4. What criteria will be used to determine if it is done? (How much or how well is it to be done?)	

Let us identify a hypothetical mission and "walk it through" as a planner might do in deriving an adequately stated mission objective. (This might be typical of the way in which a school board or legislature might hand us an issue.)

We might begin with a statement of the mission (i.e., what we want to accomplish), revising and refining this statement of intent until it has evolved to a measurable performance objective.

(1) "Improve Florida education through excellence."

We must refine this gross statement of intent until it is more precise, ultimately relating to reducing or eliminating a defined and documented need.

(2) "Increase Florida student mastery of critical skill and knowledge areas and improve self-concept of learners so they will be successful in school and life by assuring that all teachers are competent and well-trained in the content areas."

The planner has refined further—by specifying the fundamental critical skills and knowledge areas that also might be associated with how a student perceives herself, and further notes that both in-school and in-life performance is important. But it already has a solution embedded (competent, well-trained teachers) which we are not ready to select.

(3) "Measurably improve Florida in-school student mastery in reading, communication, and arithmetic, and produce an increase

in self-concept of learners. Further, students should perform at or above grade levels, and be self-sufficient and self-reliant in later life."

The planner has moved closer to rigor, completeness, and measurability and is including all major dimensions of required performance. Note that the means (process) for assisting learners to perform—competent teachers—is now missing; the focus upon the results and not the means for delivering the result has allowed this to be deleted in the objective. (The evolving changes also builds upon an intepretation of the research literature which relates self-esteem with actual performance.)

(4) Modifying statement #1 to a measurable mission objective "Increase Florida in school student performance as measured by X valid reading test and Z valid arithmetic test by at least 10 and 12 percent mean improvements, respectively, so that":

- at least 90 percent of all learners are at or above grade level
- learner self-concept will improve significantly among these learners as measured by Q valid instrument within two years
- after legal exit from the school system, at least 90 percent of all completers will be self-sufficient and self-reliant as indicated by the application of the criteria of no divorces; no unemployment; no arrests and convictions; registration for voting; no receipt of food stamps, unemployment compensation, or aid to dependent children.[10]

Statement #1 has been transformed into an acceptable objective by supplying performance criteria and the bases for evaluation. As we become more precise, we derive a mission objective that is realistic and assessable and, moreover, communicates the results (products, outputs, or outcomes) precisely with virtually no margin for misinterpretation. [Also note that as the rigor increased, there was an inclusion of outcome indicators (external self-sufficiency) as part of the mission objective. Such "moving up the results chain" can be an important contribution to an educational system's responsiveness. Of course, as was stated earlier, a mission objective may be for any result level, product, output, or outcome.]

---

[10]These criteria are oversimplified for sake of example.

Performance Requirements

Performance requirements are precise, measurable criteria for describing and determining results which form a critical element in the statement of a mission objective.

The ultimate result of the accomplishment of a mission is the creation or achievement of a specific, measurable product, output, or outcome. Performance requirements for the mission provide the exact specifications by which success (or failure) of the mission may be measured. They include the following:

- specifications stating the criteria by which the complete success of the mission objective may be measured—what the results will look like or actually do
- specifications stating the context or "ground rules" under which the result is to be produced, such as environment, costs, personnel, and other "givens"

PERFORMANCE REQUIREMENT DEFINED

A performance requirement provides the measurable criteria that specify the result which flows from completing a function. They include exactly that which the result is to do, the conditions under which it is to perform, design characteristics, and performance specifications, restrictions, or rules placed on the development of the result. They specify what the result will look like and/or accomplish, and the "given" conditions for its development, if any. An example for the specifications of a hypothetical self-instructional program might be the following:

(1) There must be learner achievement with the program to the criterion level of at least 90/90 (90 percent of learners with score 90 percent or better on the criterion test) when the resulting curriculum package is used by the specified target population and the test items are related to the defined needs.

(2) The curriculum package (program) must not cost more than $14.25 in purchase quantities of 500 or more as measured by having no audit exceptions for this item.

(3) At least eighty-five percent of all learners using the package will complete it to mastery within two hours.

(4) Two of the five school board members are opposed to this project.

(5) Accrediting standards will be met as indicated by no deficiencies being noted in the subsequent accrediting visit report.

Initially, performance requirements may be supplied by a "client" (we all have at least one boss). These "directions" represent the client's (the boss's) perceptions of what must be done, and thus her or his notions of how evaluation of success or failure will be made. A client may state requirements in nonassessable (loose, or emotional) terms. If we act on these, we take a risk of misinterpreting what result is really required and may actually accomplish something quite different from what was expected. As noted in Chapter 3, the use of needs assessment and planning partner groups plus the "hard" data can preempt an attempt to impose arbitrary requirements.

Mission analysis represents a process by which (1) partners (clients) and planner(s) may arrive at a set of measurable criteria for expected outcomes when the mission is accomplished or (2) the planner may "renegotiate" the mission with the clients if it develops that the original intent is not sufficiently functional.

The educational planner using the tools and following the steps of system analysis will have to evaluate the feasibility of requirements that are given. When stated in precise, objective, measurable terms, the performance requirements will provide the criteria for the early determination of the feasibility of accomplishing that which has been requested. (More about determining feasibility is presented in Chapter 6, Methods-Means Analysis.)

LISTING OF PERFORMANCE REQUIREMENTS

When performance requirements are being identified, we will want to keep track of them. This is best done in tabular form, associating each performance requirement, by the number of the product (termed a <u>function</u>) to be delivered, with a written statement of that performance requirement (Table 4.1).

As the system analysis identifies more and more functions the analyst will be recording performance requirements that are associated with the functions. Often, in order to track large projects, such recording might require several pages of performance requirements. When a performance requirement is the same for one function as it is for another (or the same as that stated in the mission objective and its performance requirements) it is <u>not</u> necessary to list the performance requirements over again—simply note that it is the same as those previously stated (as in Table 4.1).

TABLE 4.1 A Performance Requirements Table. Performance requirements may be
shown as a table which lists each function by its number and the
associated performance requirements for each.

Function and Number	Associated Performance Requirement
1.1 XXXXXXXXXXX XXXXXX XX XXXXXXXX XX	XXXXXXXXXXXXXXXXX XXXXXXXXXXXX XXXXXXXXXXXXXXX
1.2 XXXXXX XXX X	same as 1.0
1.4 XX XX X XXX	same as 0.0[a] and 1.3

[a]0.0 is the symbol used for the mission objective and performance requirements. There does not have
to be a new performance requirement for each function if the performance requirement from a previous
function is appropriate—it should then only be referenced (such as "same as 0.0").

Obstacles

As potential obstacles are identified in the mission analysis, they
become performance requirements; that is, they provide criteria for
specifying the characteristics or the conditions under which the
result of the mission must be accomplished. If, for instance, it is
given that "no additional funds may be spent over and above that
which is already budgeted," then this "obstacle" becomes one of the
ground rules. Even if a performance requirement is unachievable
(i.e., a constraint exists), the unfavorable requirement must be
specified and an attempt must be made to meet it before aborting or
changing the mission. Thus we see that a "constraint" arises when it
appears that a mission objective, a performance requirement, or a
set of performance requirements is not achievable. (The determination of a constraint condition is discussed in Chapter 6.)

A constraint is resolvable in several ways. First, it may be possible
to change the mission objective and/or the performance requirements; if a requirement for something no longer exists or is modified, then the specific constraint may be operationally removed. A
second possibility is to reconcile the constraint by creating a new or
different way to meet the requirement, and thus, to remove the constraint operationally. A third possibility is to reach a "compromise"
relative to the performance requirement and its achievement. This
compromise might be said to amount to bringing an out-of-bounds
condition into tolerance. This reconciliation of a constraint might be
exemplified by the easing of a specification that had been set for an
objective (e.g., changing a performance requirement of "a mean of 75
with a standard deviation of 12" to "a mean of 75 with a standard deviation of 15"). In this example, the basic requirement remains, but

there is a variation granted in the "spread" in the student's performance. A <u>fourth</u> possibility for dealing with a constraint is to stop—
if you can't get there from here, why go farther?

The identification of a constraint[11] requires decisions to (1) change
the mission objective and/or its performance requirements (and possibly not meet the needs), (2) call on creativity and make or synthesize a new and responsive methods-means, or (3) stop because it does
not make sense to proceed with a problem if there are positive in-
dications that the effort would be a failure. When we have identified
a constraint, we know then that moving on without change will risk
a higher-than-acceptable probability of failure.

Putting Specificity into a Mission Objective

In Chapter 3 it was noted that an assessment of educational needs
would provide hard data concerning problem dimensions of "what is"
and "what is required." Hard empirical data indicate that measurable criteria have been identified to document both the beginning
and the end characteristics of a given problem area.

The job of writing a mission objective and its associated performance requirements without hard data from a needs assessment
obliges the educational planner to obtain valid data on the problem
and characteristics that will allow the determination of the relative
success or failure of the mission. This additional job for the planner
or designer is vital to the success of the educational system planning
effort. As Mager (1975) so ably put it, "If you don't know where you
are going, you might end up someplace else."

It also should be noted that a need which has been selected for reduction or elimination (the problem) might have several elements, or
parts. A mission objective might relate to accomplishing a whole array of related results.

One may set objectives in precise measurable terms only to find
that precision does not assure validity. Further assurance of validity
is furnished by the needs assessment data. By referring to the measurable gaps between what is and what should be, criteria for objectives may be obtained. Also, some planners may find it difficult to
move from a general statement of a mission intent to the detailed
performance requirements involved in completing a useful mission
analysis. In this instance, consider the possible usefulness of a conceptual pyramid (Figure 4.1) where the analysis proceeds from gross

[11]Constraints and their reconciliation are fully discussed in Chapter 6. Their importance is best understood when related to the methods-means analysis.

LINCOLN CHRISTIAN COLLEGE AND SEMINARY

78124

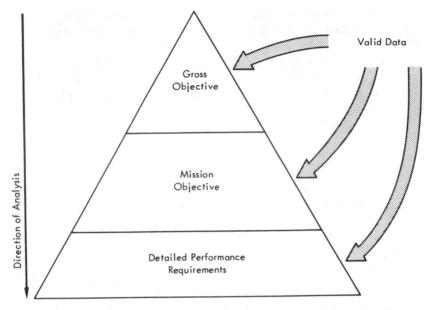

Figure 4.1. A possible process for deriving relevant and detailed mission objectives and their associated performance requirements from general, global intentions.

objectives to a mission objective and then to the detailed perform-ance requirements to describe the characteristics of the result of the mission. This is a gradual process for achieving increasing spe-cificity and precision while moving from the general to the specific.

Viewed in this manner, the mission objective and its associated performance requirements actually form a unitary package that states what is to be accomplished and how one can determine when the job has been completed. Without the performance requirements attached, a mission objective seldom supplies the criterion for evalu-ation and thus will not give the educational planner the information required to derive a relevant and practical plan for achieving the ob-jective and its associated performance requirements. Together, then, the mission objective and the performance requirements provide the starting referent and the specifications for system analysis.

A TAXONOMY OF RESULTS

Sometimes we know more about some results than we do about others. For example, sometimes we can only name something, or on-ly know that some things are greater than, equal to, or less than something else. Other times, we can measure something with great-er reliability.

There is a taxonomy of results which will allow us to identify both the relative reliability of our consequences, but also to distinguish between goals and objectives. There are four scales of measurement:

Nominal—naming something ("cat," "Jan," "creativity")

Ordinal—determining that things are greater than, equal to, or less than other things ("John is stronger than Bob;" "this sunset painting is better than the seascape, and both are better than the still life over here")

Interval—stipulating an arbitrary zero-point to start the measurement and specifying equal scale distances (means and standard deviations on an intelligence test, temperature in centigrade)

Ratio—operating from a known zero-point and with equal scale distances (temperature in Kelvin, weight, distance)

Using these for types of measurement (with ratio the most reliable, and nominal the least), a taxonomy of results including a descriptor of each is shown in Table 4.2.

the mission profile

The second part of mission analysis is the mission profile. The planning effort so far has yielded (1) what is to be accomplished (the mission objective), and (2) the performance requirements for the mission.

The planner now must proceed from where one is to where one should be. This involves what is to be accomplished, not "how" and not "who will actually implement any intervention or method."

The products that must be completed and delivered in order to accomplish the overall result, regardless of how it gets done, are termed functions. When the major functions of a mission are identified and placed in logical sequence, they constitute the mission

TABLE 4.2 A taxonomy of results.

Scale of Measurement	Result Descriptor
Nominal Ordinal	Goal, aim, purpose
Interval Ratio	Objective, performance specification

profile—a management plan identifying the products that must be completed, the sequence in which they are to be completed, and the order of their completion required to accomplish a mission. Thus the mission profile represents the functional path for achievement of the end result, usually an outcome. The discrete functions within the mission profile may vary from two to N functions, depending on the complexity of the mission.

Using a Discrepancy Analysis in Preparing the Mission Profile

In an earlier discussion, it was noted that the identification of needs constituted a part of the needs assessment (or discrepancy analysis). This notion of a discrepancy analysis appears continuously as part of system analysis, for in several instances, we want to identify what is to be done to eliminate a discrepancy (i.e., to meet a need). (Please note that a discrepancy is not the same as a deficiency. Too much of something may lead to a discrepancy, but is obviously not a deficiency.)

In needs assessment we have identified "where we should be." This statement and data provide the mission objective and its performance requirements. Now we must plan the path-of-products for getting from our current results to our required results, and we should derive the mission profile—a management plan identifying what is to be done to get us from the "what is" area of our needs assessment statement to "what should be." The mission profile provides the identification of the functions to be accomplished and the order in which they are to be completed. The successful completion of these functions will eliminate the discrepancy identified in our first and most significant discrepancy analysis, the needs assessment.

A mission profile is made up of the orderly progression of products to be completed and delivered.

How Is a Mission Profile Derived?

Step 1—Obtain the mission objective and the performance requirements that tell where we will be when we have completed the mission. Next describe the status quo. A mission profile, as we know, is derived to identify what is to be completed to get us from "what is" to "what is required." The mission profile will list the necessary functions (products, or results), and define the logical order in which the functions are to be performed and completed. Be sure to leave out how any of the functions will be done. Mission analysis deals only with identifying "what" is to be completed—products—not methods and means to be employed. Identify and list the first function to be completed.

Step 2—When the first major function in the mission profile has been identified, the question is then asked, "What is the next logical step to complete—product to be delivered?" The next function is then identified and listed. This process is continued until the planner has moved from the <u>first</u> function of the mission profile to the <u>last</u> function required to meet and accomplish the mission objective and its performance requirements.[12]

Step 3—When all the major functions in the mission profile have been identified, they are reexamined against the needs, the mission objective, and the performance requirements in order to assure internal consistency among the functions and external validity based on the needs. The mission profile must be both complete and relatable to the needs.

It should be emphasized that the process of check and recheck is performed throughout the entire analysis process. It is necessary to review the scope and order of identified functions to determine whether any have been omitted or if unnecessary ones are included, and to assure that they are in proper sequence. Some functions may be best unified under a larger function, for example, and these should be identified in a collective manner. Examination of the mission profile also may uncover performance requirements that were previously unidentified or overlooked.

Step 4—Once internal consistency has been determined and assured, arrange the functions in a flow chart, an orderly array of rectangles or squares, then connect the graphic "blocks" with solid lines so that the arrow points follow the flow of the functions from the first to the last.[13]

As the analysis proceeds, new data may come to light, which in turn might alter the mission profile. System analysis is a dynamic process and, through the utilization of newly uncovered data, the mission objective, the performance requirements, and/or the mission profile might be subject to change. <u>The analyst must be ready and</u>

---

[12]In performing a mission (and a function) analysis, the planner may, if she prefers, reverse this normal chronological process and move from the end to the beginning. In this "back-to-front mode" the mission objective defines the end; it states where you will be when you have accomplished the mission, and this becomes a "known." Then the analyst begins with the "known" and works backward until arriving at the initial state.

[13]More detailed information concerning flow chart preparation may be found in Chapter 5, Function Analysis.

willing to change the profile at any time—it should be "cast in wax, not in concrete"!

The overall process involved in a mission analysis is shown in Figure 4.2 in the form of a mission profile. The major functions appear as described in this chapter, and the relations among the various functions are made clear. These functions are: (1.0) state the mission objective, then (2.0) state the performance requirements in measurable terms which derive from the mission objective, (3.0) derive the management plan which shows the major functions required to accomplish the mission—the mission profile, and (4.0) revise any or all of the previous steps as required to maintain consistency between the original requirement and the steps and products derived in performing a mission analysis. Not all the steps discussed in this chapter are shown in Figure 4.2; these represent subordinate functions to be performed and constitute subfunctions (this is taken up in detail in the next chapter). Notice that the mission profile constitutes a management plan (or road map) in that it sets forth the major functions involved in getting from "what is" to "what is required."

A hypothetical partial mission (based on Corrigan et al., 1967) will be useful for the sake of helping to explain the steps and tools of system analysis. In this example, a giant hypothetical problem was to be tackled. Figure 4.3 represents a possible mission profile for the tentative and equally hypothetical mission objective and associated performance requirements, which were to identify the 50 highest priority needs in education, identify possible cost-effective solutions, and implement projects to reduce or eliminate each need with mea-

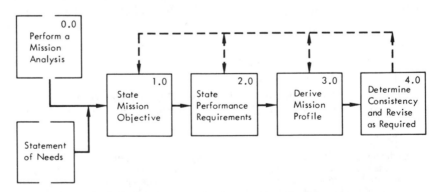

Figure 4.2. A sample mission profile for accomplishing the mission of "perform a mission analysis." This example shows that there are four basic functions (or steps) that may be involved in performing a mission analysis. Note that revision of any previous function is possible; the dotted lines show feedback of data for the purpose of revision.

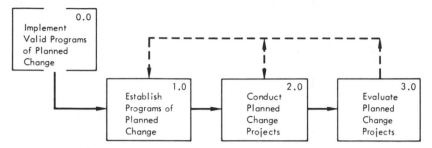

Figure 4.3. A hypothetical mission profile for implementing valid programs of planned change in education.

surable reduction in the needs as judged by (1) the Secretary of education and (2) at least 35 of the superintendents of public instruction of the 50 states, including New York, California, Texas, Illinois, Pennsylvania, Massachusetts, and Florida. Such measurable reduction in needs must be evident and judged as operating satisfactorily within five years of the initiation of the effort. Funding is to be obtained from both federal and local sources.

The three major functions identified in the mission profile are: (1) establish programs of planned change, (2) conduct planned change projects, and (3) evaluate planned change projects. Revision throughout the project (called "formative evaluation") and at the completion of the third function (called "summative evaluation") in this mission profile is indicated by the dotted line, denoting the availability of performance data for revision to any or all previous functions and tasks. (These types of evaluation are two of the three identified by Scriven, 1967.)

It should be emphasized that not all mission profiles look alike. Recall the basic six-step problem-solving model which shows a mission profile for identifying and solving problems, and review the mission profile presented in Chapter 2 which showed the functions to be performed in designing instructional materials using a system approach (Figure 2.2, p. 34). Figure 4.4, for instance, is a mission profile developed for a planning effort for the hypothetical Gotham School District which is used as an example in Chapter 8.

Each function in a mission profile identifies a product—an interim, building-block result—required for the partial fulfillment of the mission objective and its performance requirements. The total of the products identified in a mission profile will yield the larger, overall results specified in the mission objective and its performance requirements. (Development and construction of flow charts such as mission profiles are detailed in the next chapter.)

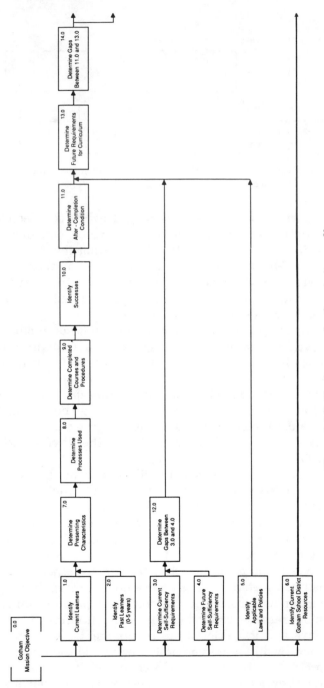

Figure 4.4 (left). An example of a mission profile.

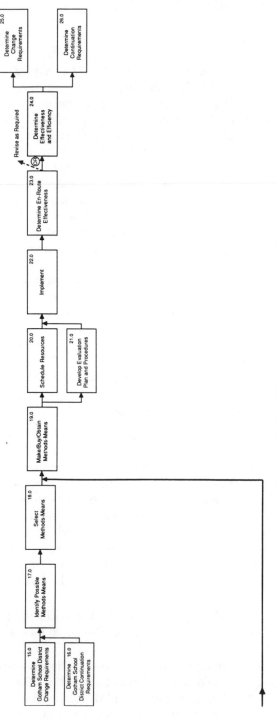

Figure 4.4 (right). An example of a mission profile.

summary

A mission is the statement of intent about the overall result (usually an outcome, but possibly an output or product) we want to accomplish. It should be based on documented needs.

A mission objective states the mission precisely in terms of a measurable performance specification, stating <u>what</u> is to be accomplished, who or what will display the final result; and under what conditions the accomplishment may be observed.

The performance requirements specify measurable products, outputs, or outcomes (results) of the mission and set forth the specifications and boundaries within which the mission must be achieved. Together, the mission objective and the performance requirements state "where we are going and how we know when we have arrived." (The needs assessment told us "why we should go there.")

In a logically ordered sequence, the mission profile identifies all the major functions that must be performed to finish the mission and produce the required result satisfying the specifications in the performance requirements. This is the major pathway for meeting the mission objective. With the completion of the mission objective, its performance requirements, and the mission profile, the educational planner has completed the mission analysis. Now the stage is set for the second phase of system analysis: function analysis.

The following steps are involved in performing a mission analysis:

(1) Obtain needs data from needs assessment and the problem statements that derived from the assessment.

(2) Derive the mission objective and the performance requirements so that it is possible to answer, in measurable performance terms, the following questions: (a) what result is to be demonstrated? (b) by whom or what is the result to be demonstrated? (c) Under what conditions is it to be demonstrated? and (d) what criteria will be used to determine if it has been accomplished? These statements of "where we are going" and "how we know when we have arrived" form the mission objective <u>and</u> the performance requirements.

(3) Verify that the mission objective and the performance requirements accurately represent the problem selected based on the documented needs.

(4) Prepare the mission profile, which shows the major functions required to get from "what is" to "what should be." Remember that the mission profile is a management plan setting forth the functions (or products) to be completed which are necessary to

eliminate the discrepancy that constitutes the problem. Each function identified will: (a) Identify a result (product) that is to be accomplished and delivered; (b) Be graphically positioned to show its relative independence from the other functions in the mission profile; (c) Be numbered in sequence to show the relation between each function and every other function; (d) Be joined by solid lines with arrows to denote the exact flow and the relation between each function and all the other functions.

(5) Check the mission analysis to make sure that all elements are presented, that they are in the correct order, that they are consistent with the mission objective and the performance requirements, and that they are consistent with the needs selected and the associated problem statements. Make any necessary changes based on the needs assessment data.

glossary

Mission   the overall job to be done to meet the identified and documented needs.

Mission objective   an objective that measurably states the specifications for determining when we have successfully reached where we should be. This performance objective has four elements: (1) what results are to be demonstrated, (2) by whom or what is the result to be demonstrated, (3) under what conditions it is to be demonstrated, and (4) what criteria will be used to determine if it has been accomplished?

Mission profile   a management plan depicting, in flow chart form, the functions (or products) necessary to get from where one is to the satisfactory completion of the mission (as measured by the mission objective and its associated performance requirements).

Taxonomy of results   any result which is measurable on a nominal or ordinal scale is called a "goal," "aim," or "purpose," and any result measurable on an interval or ratio scale is called an "objective," or "performance specification."

exercises

1. Produce a mission objective, performance requirements, and a mission profile for an educational problem of your choice which will meet all of the criteria for these elements:
    a. What results are to be demonstrated?
    b. By whom or what are the results to be demonstrated?

    c. Under what conditions is the result to be demonstrated?

    d. What criteria will be used to determine if it—the mission—has been accomplished?

This four-part mission objective will state the exact outcome (or output, or product) of the mission and contain the criterion basis for evaluation. In the case of curriculum design, the mission must be learner-oriented.

Performance requirements will contain product specifications, restrictions, and performance characteristics of the results to be accomplished and will identify measurement criteria.

The mission profile will identify the major functions to be performed in order to successfully accomplish the mission. Each function must appear in its logical order. The mission profile must be internally consistent with the mission objective and the performance requirements; if implemented, it should result in the achievement of the stated mission objective and performance requirements.

Answer the following correctly:

Fill in the Blanks

2. A mission objective must fulfill the following requirements:

    a. _____

    b. _____

    c. (for curriculum design): _____

3. We call the description of the result of the mission, its specification, tolerances, characteristics, and restrictions the _____. These tell what the final result must _____ and/or

_____.

4. The mission profile is a sequence of _____ representing the major milestones that must be passed to accomplish the mission. It is considered to be the _____ to mission achievement.

5. Before the mission profile can be derived, the _____ _____ and _____ must be identified.

Answer the Following Questions

6. What is the role of the mission objective?

7. What is the role of the performance requirements?

8. State how the mission objective, performance requirements, and mission profile relate to one another and collectively; in what order they are derived; and why this order must be maintained.

9. What is the relation between the mission analysis and what is to follow in a complete system analysis?

10. Design a criterion measure for the performance objective on page 97 that would test the performance of the learner in terms of the stated objective.

11. Write ten objective test questions that would test the relevant concepts in the mission analysis chapter.

CHAPTER 5

function analysis[14]

A FUNCTION IS one of several related products (or results) contributing to a larger one. It is a collection of completed jobs or tasks—delivered results—necessary to achieve a specified objective or bring about a given product, output, or outcome. Each of the functions works together with other functions to accomplish the mission of the system. Analysis is the process of breaking something down into its constituent component parts and identifying that which each part does independently and in contribution to the larger whole's purposes. Function analysis identifies that which must be accomplished in order to meet an objective.

In performing a function analysis, the system planner continues the planning that began with the needs assessment and the mission analysis (including the mission objective, performance requirements, and the mission profile). In so doing, the planner is deriving and identifying additional "whats"—the products identified in the mission profile—that must be completed in order to assure the successful achievement of the mission objective and performance requirements. Notice that here, as in all system analysis, the concern is only with the "whats" and not the "hows." In doing a function analysis, as with mission analysis, the analyst is identifying <u>what</u> has to be done as well as the <u>order</u> in which the products are to be completed. Some examples of functions[15] as they might be stated in a function analysis are:

- Identify functions.
- Complete function analysis.

[14]And Task Analysis as an option.

[15]Actually, these <u>might</u> also be correctly stated as <u>completed</u> in order to communicate the product-nature of a function (e.g., "delivered district budget;" "collected data"). To emphasize that we are planning what has to be accomplished, however, examples used here and elsewhere show functions <u>to be</u> completed.

113

- Deliver district budget.
- Hire teachers.
- Collect data.
- Summarize data.

Function analysis proceeds from the top-level (mission profile) functions, one at a time, in an orderly manner. The product of any function analysis is the identification of an array of functions and subfunctions (down to the lowest level of relevance), including the determination of the interrelations required to achieve a mission. Examine the following hypothetical problem situation:

Need—Z percent of California public school graduates earn G percent less than a subsistence wage, and this Z percent should earn a subsistence wage or greater. Of this Z percent only 23 percent of them are literate.

Problem—At least 95 percent of the Z percent of California school graduates should earn at least a subsistence wage.

Solution—Improve reading skills by using the "X" method of reading content improvement.

Critique—The solution is proposed before an analysis has been performed to determine requirements and functions. Problem solving jumped from the problem to "how" without determining the "whats."

Function analysis proceeds from the results of the mission analysis to a precise statement naming the functions that must be performed in order to solve the problem. Following is a hypothetical sequence.

Need—"Q percent" of third graders in the Rojas School District read below "P" level, and this Q percent should read at the "P" level or better.

Problem—By June 1, reading skills of third graders in the Rojas School District will be at the "P" level or better.

Functions—Determine reading skill and subskill areas; determine teaching/reading training resources; learner learning strategies, learner and teacher values; teacher competencies, etc.

The function analysis process (1) analyzes what should be accomplished, and (2) gives the proper order of subordinate, constituent, or lower order accomplishments (e.g., jobs or tasks), in order to achieve the mission objective and its associated performance requirements (and thus resolves the problem):

- It analyzes.
- It identifies.
- It orders.

levels of function analysis

It was previously mentioned that functions and related subfunctions are identified through the process of function analysis. Recalling the definition of a function as one of a group of results (or products) contributing to a larger result (or product), a key to the levels of function analysis may be found in the words "larger result" (or product). Larger products (or outputs, or outcomes) may be referred to as <u>higher level functions</u>. The highest level function is the mission itself, and all other functions derive from that highest level or overall function.

One useful way of viewing the relation between mission analysis and function analysis is in terms of a matrix, with the mission analysis forming the "top" of the matrix and the function analysis as the "depth" dimension. In performing a function analysis, we are filling in the "depth" or additional dimensions of the mission analysis. Greatly simplified, such a matrix would resemble Figure 5.1. The function analysis is a vertical expansion of the mission analysis—each element in the mission profile is composed of functions, and it is the role of the function analyst to identify, for each function

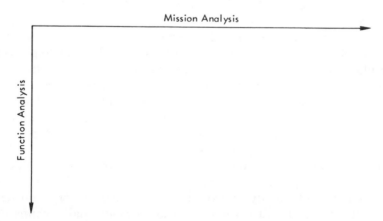

Figure 5.1. Function analysis may be seen as a vertical expansion of the mission analysis.

named in the mission analysis and depicted in the mission profile, all the subfunctions and their interrelations.

The function analysis, then, is "filling in the details." It includes the specification of requirements and interrelations among the identified subfunctions for each product in the mission profile.

As detailed later in this chapter, an important aspect of the further analysis is the identification of the ways in which the subfunctions interrelate with other subfunctions. When there are interrelations between different major functions identified in the mission profile—or with their subfunctions—these interrelations are called "interactions." Because a successful system has many parts (or subsystems) which must work together, a critical part of system analysis is concerned with identifying interactions and planning for the successful meshing of parts.

"Smaller" contributing products are called lower-level functions or subfunctions. The analyst looks at the higher-level functions (beginning with the functions identified in the mission profile) in much the same manner as he would use a microscope with varying degrees of magnification power to examine a natural phenomenon (Corrigan and Kaufman, 1966). A low magnification power would show a larger field, and a higher magnification power would show a small field but with more detail.

In using this analysis "microscope," the planner keeps the analysis at one particular level at any given time. Looking through the "microscope" one attends first to the identification of the overall functions (or higher-level functions), thereafter focusing at the same level of magnitude until all functions of equal magnitude have been identified. Since the mission profile represents the primary functions which, when accomplished, will yield the result specified in the mission objective, the mission profile level is called the "top level." The planner then uses a "higher power of magnification" and analyzes each high-level function to identify the lower-level functions (or subfunctions) which collectively would accomplish each top-level function. Only when the planner is satisfied that all the subfunctions have been identified and that they are internally consistent with all the previous steps does she proceed to lower levels.

Another way of understanding levels of function analysis would be to use the analogy of analyzing a map of the United States. The highest level to be analyzed would be the whole country; the next level, the states; a still lower level, the counties; and perhaps the lowest level, the cities and towns. (If one required more detailed information, the cities and towns could be further broken down into districts, neighborhoods, blocks, residences, buildings, parking lots and parks, etc.) In performing a function analysis by levels, the analyst makes every attempt not to confuse the functions of counties with states, or cities with counties.

A function is something to be achieved, completed, delivered. For example: "Provide learners with function analysis skills." To identify the function as discrete, and to show its relation to other functions that might be identified, we put in a numbered box:

```
┌─────────────────────────┐
│              1.0        │
│                         │
│  Provide Learners       │
│  with                   │
│  Function Analysis      │
│  Skills                 │
└─────────────────────────┘
```

We have derived "provide learners with function analysis skills" (or block 1.0) from a hypothetical needs assessment and mission analysis. It should be noted that it is the first of several prime functions in this hypothetical mission profile, so we call this prime function a top-level function. Consider the two following examples:

```
A ┌─────────────────┐    B ┌─────────────────────┐
  │           1.0   │      │              1.0    │
  │                 │      │                     │
  │ Function Analysis│      │ Provide Learners    │
  │                 │      │ with                │
  │                 │      │ Function Analysis   │
  │                 │      │ Skills              │
  └─────────────────┘      └─────────────────────┘
```

Box A does not tell what is to be accomplished; it could be interpreted as "read about" or even "ignore" the stated function. Box B is a properly stated top-level function, revealing what has to be delivered, or accomplished. A function shows a product (or subproduct) to be achieved and as such is really a "miniature" mission objective with the same properties and characteristics.

The next step in demonstrating this hypothetical function analysis is to analyze the functions necessary to "provide learners with function analysis skills." This requires the analyst to "drop" to a first level below the top (or mission profile level) function; in other words perform a vertical expansion[16] (see Figure 5.2).

---

[16]Such a "dropping down" and expanding is sometimes referred to as *breaking-out* a function.

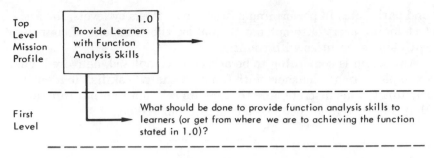

Figure 5.2. "Breaking-out" or expanding a top-level function.

It is possible to keep analyzing "lower-level" functions that are necessary to perform higher-level functions until there are a number of "layers" or levels in the function analysis.[17] Function analysis may be continued until (a) one is confident that there is enough specificity to assure getting the required results, and (b) any further breaking-down would require the identifying of processes.

Figure 5.3 illustrates the numbering format. In actual function analysis, each function block would contain the statement of the function <u>and</u> the appropriate reference number. Since the overall function is the mission objective, it is labeled 0.0 in a flow diagram.

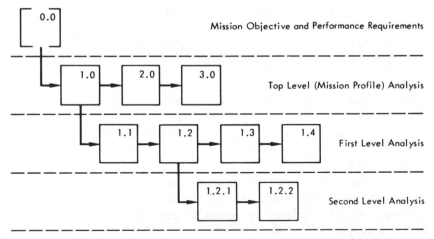

Figure 5.3. A hypothetical expansion (starting with a mission objective).

[17]Only the analysis of function 1.0 is shown and then only to the second level. In actual planning and function analysis, all top-level functions are analyzed to as many levels as required.

the rules of function analysis

The rules of function analysis are not designed to make the process difficult, but to:

- keep track of where one is and show requirements for getting to where one should be
- allow clear communication with others

Rule 1—All blocks are rectangular or square and are of the same size.

Rule 2—Each block contains a statement of a result to be accomplished or delivered.

Rule 3—Function blocks are consistently connected as in Figure 5.4. To see if it works, see Figure 5.5

Rule 4—A decimal system is used in numbering, and a decimal point and a number are added for each level analyzed (Figure 5.6). Also, all blocks are numbered in the upper right-hand corner.

Rule 5—If a higher level function cannot be broken down into two or more functions, don't break it down further.

Rule 6—Functions are connected with solid lines with an arrow tip to show forward flow. Revision pathways are shown with dotted lines and an arrow tip. When a choice is to be made among two or more paths, a circled "or" between the paths is used to signal that choice.

When you have done a function analysis, drawing function blocks and connecting them according to the rules, you have prepared a function flow block diagram. A function flow block diagram graphically reveals the order, stages, and interrelationships of "what" has to be accomplished. Done properly, a function analysis will answer the following:

(1) What has to be accomplished or delivered?

(2) In what order must the functions be completed?

(3) What component functions (or products) compose each higher-level function?

(4) What are the relations among the functions?

A function analysis for the function: "Provide learners with function analysis skills," (1.0 in Figure 5.7) might be set up as in Figure 5.7.

Functions Are Products, Not Processes or Means

When first performing a function analysis, one often inappropriately lists means for performing the function rather than showing

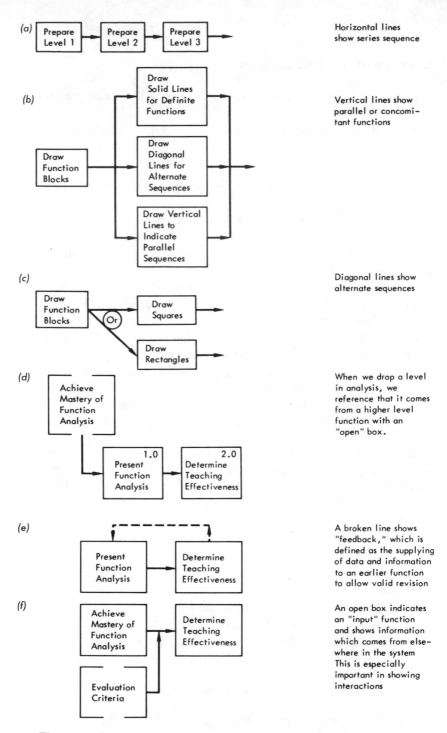

Figure 5.4. Some formulating conventions for system analysis flow charts.

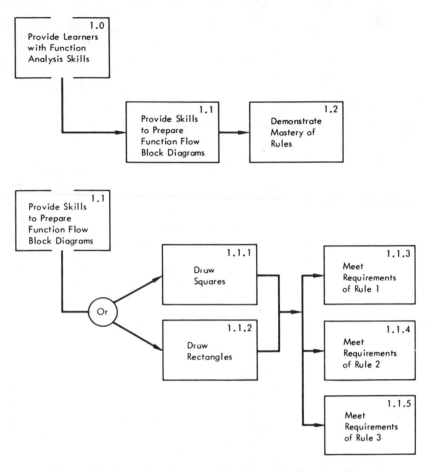

Figure 5.5. Some flow charting rules depicted in flow chart format.

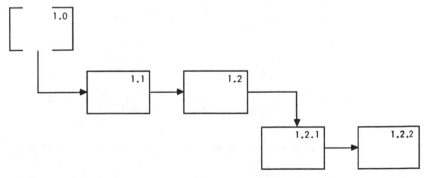

Figure 5.6. 1.0: top level (a zero after the decimal always indicates top level); 1.X: first level (identified by a number, a decimal point, and another number other than zero); 1.X.Y: second level (a number, a decimal point, a second number, another decimal point, and another number).

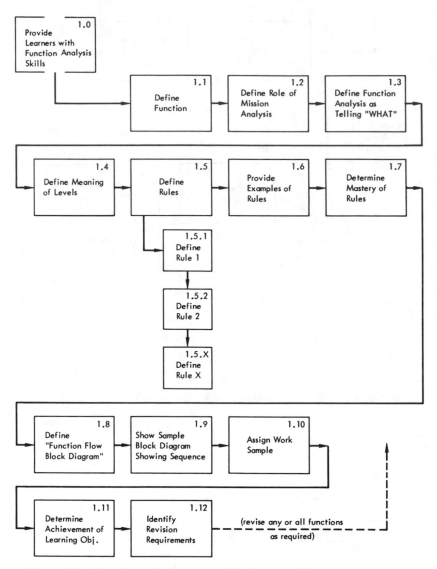

Figure 5.7. A flow chart showing a possible "break-out" of a top-level function.

the end product or result. For instance, an <u>erroneous</u> example might be:

> Administer the W.K.
> Roberts Self-Concept
> Instrument

This example tells <u>how</u> to obtain self-concept information (use the hypothetical W. K. Roberts Self-Concept Instrument), not what the resulting product should be. Throughout an analysis, when you find solutions "creeping in," ask yourself, "What is it that this method or means will give me when I am through?" Or, "Why do I want to give that particular test?" By asking this type of question you will be able to determine the product that you are seeking, rather than backing yourself into a less-than-optimal process or solution. Thus a better function statement is:

> Determine
> Individual
> Self-Concept

One of the critical reasons for performing a system analysis in general and a function analysis in particular is to free ourselves from the possible how-we-have-always-done-it "straitjackets" of the past with new, responsive, responsible, and better ways of doing things.

Every Level of System Analysis Is Related to Every Other Level

The process of system analysis really starts with the assessment of needs where discrepancies between "what is" and "what is required" are identified. The latter dimension provides the basis (or core) for the mission objective, thus furnishing the connection or "bridge" between needs assessment and mission analysis:

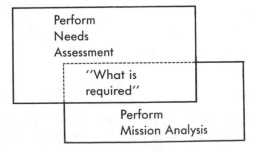

The mission analysis identifies the mission objective, the performance requirements and the mission profile, and the levels of analysis are interrelated in a logical, internally consistent manner. The mission profile (the top level of function analysis) thus bridges, or links, mission analysis and function analysis as shown by the following:

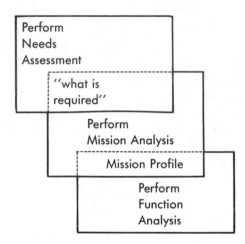

Perform
Needs
Assessment

"what is
required"

Perform
Mission Analysis

Mission Profile

Perform
Function
Analysis

a few tips on conducting an analysis

Analysis is the process of breaking things down into their component parts and noting the interrelations between the parts and the contributions of the parts to the whole and its purposes.

Analyzing Something

Try <u>listing</u> constituent components during analysis. For instance, in order to drive to work, you must eventually perform all the following activities (if you have both a garage and an automobile):

- Open garage.
- Walk out door.
- Start car.
- Find car keys.
- Drive car.
- Get to work.

Now list the components in the order in which they would logically occur (find keys, walk out door, etc.). Scan your list critically, asking,

"What have I missed?" (How about: back car out of garage, say good-bye to family, close garage door, get in car, park car, lock car, get out of car, etc.?)

Keep an open mind and be willing and ready to revise. Figure 5.8 illustrates how the get-to-work function may be diagrammed; note that two or more simultaneous functions may be shown in "parallel."

Determining Analysis Levels

Keep the analysis within its own level. For example, not all the components listed below are true constituents of the get-to-work function:

- Get dressed.
- Shine shoes.
- Brush teeth.
- Eat breakfast.
- Get to work.

(Shining shoes and brushing teeth are components of "get dressed" and would be analyzed as being part of the "get dressed" level.)

In doing a function analysis try to find one more component that may have been omitted. It is easy to complete Figure 5.9. Keep drawing blocks for components—even if you don't know what they will contain—surprisingly often you will think of something. Constantly ask yourself "why?" or "what else?" Question everything. If it isn't right, make it right!

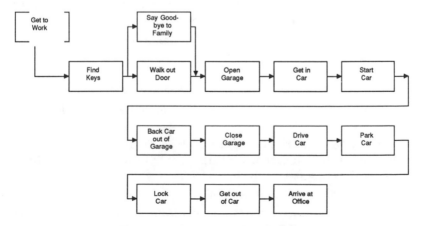

Figure 5.8. Get-to-work flow diagram.

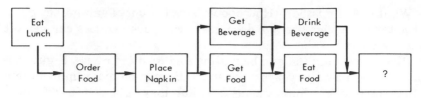

Figure 5.9. Find the omitted component.

performing a function analysis

The following procedure is suggested for performing a function analysis:

(A) The function analysis proceeds from the mission analysis. Below is a product-level example of a <u>hypothetical</u> mission analysis which is the starting point for the function analysis.

Mission Objective—Identify all the "creatively gifted" students in Carron High School by September 1, and increase their concept formation and inductive reasoning abilities significantly (.05 level of confidence or beyond) as measured by the valid H. Mayer Inquiry Inventory.

Performance Requirements

Performance requirements state both criteria for successful completion as well as the "ground-rules" or conditions under which the results must be accomplished:

(1) The identified students must meet the minimum standards set by the state for any program funding.

(2) Each student identified must be accompanied by a parent-approved written justification based on established criteria (an IEP—Individual Education Plan).

(3) Project must be completed in one school year.

(4) Budget is $28,000, excluding school personnel available.

(5) Personnel available are:
    a. one psychometrist (M.A.) in District employ.
    b. one teacher in school writing master's thesis on characteristics of creatively gifted children.

(6) Total school enrollment is 2000.

(7) Access to cumulative records is available to authorized personnel only.

(8) Maximum of three periods of class time interruption is allowable per student.

(9) The H. Mayer Instrument is available only to credentialed counselors or registered psychologists.

(B) Begin with top level function 1.0 (see Figure 5.10) and ask, "What steps must be taken (by someone or something) to accomplish 1.0?" Just as the functions to be performed in the mission profile were identified, start by identifying the product for that function[18] (see Figure 5.11).

Preparing the function flow block diagrams uses, once again, the concept of a discrepancy analysis. Each function identified in the mission profile represents a subproduct to be achieved. In function analysis we determine exactly the subfunctions (or sub-subproducts) required to accomplish that higher-level function using a discrepancy analysis to show the difference between where we are now and what has to be accomplished to eliminate that discrepancy. The process is like doing a "mini-mission analysis" at each level of the function analysis procedure. Each function has its own objective and its own performance requirements, and we can draw a mini-mission profile for accomplishing each function.

The processes utilized in the various levels of system analysis differ only in degree, not in kind—we repeat the same process over and over in more detail as we identify and define all the requirements for meeting the need and selected problem. The elements, again, are:

(1) Identify what is required for each function or subfunction.

(2) Identify the status quo for each function and subfunction.

(3) Identify functions and or subfunctions necessary to meet the requirements for completion of that function (or subfunction) and additional performance requirements for the achievement of that function.

(4) List the functions (or subfunctions) in their proper chronology so that sequence and interrelations may be determined visually (this uses the tools and formatting of function flow block diagramming).

---

[18]The analyst at this point and throughout the analysis phase is assuming a role similar to that of composer. Being in this segment of the planning phase should not be confused with the doing phase. To successfully play the role of planner, assume that on completion of the planning phase you are leaving the area and that your plans will be carried out by others without your assistance; you want to assure that they will not be apt to confuse the identification of what must be done with the actual doing of it.

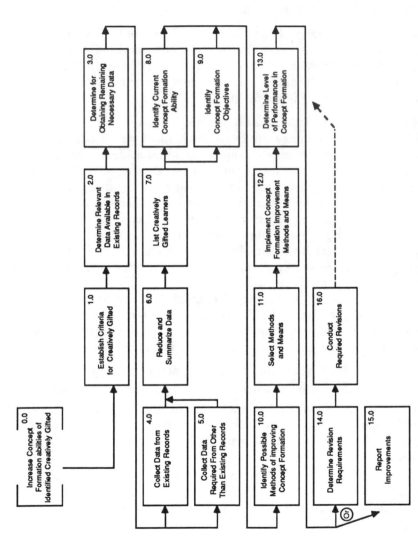

Figure 5.10 A possible mission profile for identifying gifted learners and improving concept formation.

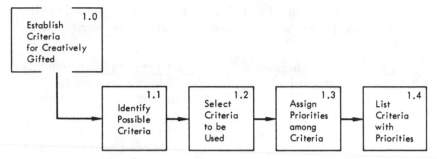

Figure 5.11. Function analysis: note that the box for 1.0 is open, indicating that it is a reference function.

(C) Proceed with function 2.0, then 3.0, and so on, until the top level of analysis (mission profile) has been completed and any additional performance requirements have been listed by function number.

(D) Check all the previous functions that have been "broken out" with the mission objective and performance requirements. This process represents a check for internal consistency, a broad inquiry whether it is still feasible to continue, and an examination of the analysis to determine if more performance requirements exist. When the product seems <u>temporarily</u> satisfactory, proceed to another level of analysis.

(E) In the same manner as in step B (p. 127) attend to the breakout of functions necessary to accomplish function 1.1, then 1.2, etc. Figure 5.12 shows the first-level analysis of function 1.2 into

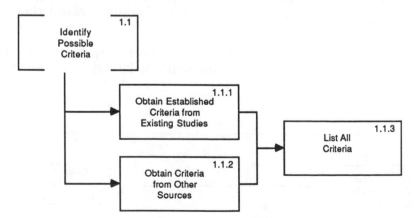

Figure 5.12. First-step analysis of 1.1: "Identify possible criteria."

its lower-level functions. The following format is suggested for listing additional performance requirements uncovered during function analysis:

Function and Number	Performance Requirements
1.1.1. Obtain established criteria.	a. Existing data contained in studies on file at the district library and county library, which have been validated, will be used exclusively.
1.1.2. Obtain criteria from other sources.	a. "Other" sources will be approved by Assistant Superintendent for Instruction. b. Project must be completed by February.
1.1.3. List all criteria.	a. Same as 1.1.1 and 1.1.2.

(F) When the first level has been completed, check for internal consistency as in the top level. Check back and forth, upward and downward, continually asking, "Can it realistically happen this way and still meet the mission objective and its performance requirements?" It must also be determined whether all the components (functions) interact properly. Do the mission and the analysis make sense? Can it work? Figure 5.13 displays the circular checking process.

(G) Continue downward to the succeeding lower levels of analysis (cf. Figure 5.14 as a generic example) until the functions are finite enough to take on the appearance of individual units rather than sets or groups of actions.

When this level of analysis has been reached, stop the breaking down here. In most educational planning it is only necessary to break functions down to this level.

Figure 5.13. The "circular" checking process.

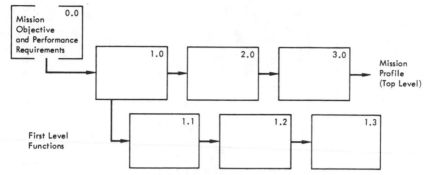

Figure 5.14. System analysis proceeds in a layer-by-layer fashion.

(In some cases, however, one might wish to continue to analyze into individual units of products, perhaps to define curriculum and course requirements. This level of analysis is called "task analysis" and will be discussed as an option later in this chapter.)

(H) Prepare a summary flow diagram of functions at various levels, in the order in which the functions are performed, and showing critical feedback and interaction pathways. (Be prepared to revise it.) List all additional performance requirements separately by function number. Often, in a large analysis, parts of the analysis at lower levels are performed separately and then brought together. The success of the resulting mesh (or interface) depends, in part, on adequate review of the final flow diagram to make sure that all subsystems interact properly. Always be critical—question and require justification for everything.

The flow charts provided in Figures 5.14 and 5.15 show partial function "break-outs" for typical examples. Figure 5.14 derives from the mission profile in Chapter 4, and Figure 5.16 from some of the functions shown in the plans for the hypothetical Gotham School District mission profiles provided in Chapter 8.

The function analysis shown in Figure 5.14 (as an example only) breaks down function number 12.0 into the first level of analysis, and (sub)functions 12.2 and 12.3 are broken down to the second level of analysis.

There is often the misconception that the "top level" analysis is mission analysis and the next level of analysis is function analysis; this is not so! Function analysis occurs at all levels, including the mission analysis level. Actually, a mission analysis is a special case of a function analysis. The functions identified at the mission level are further broken out, level by level.

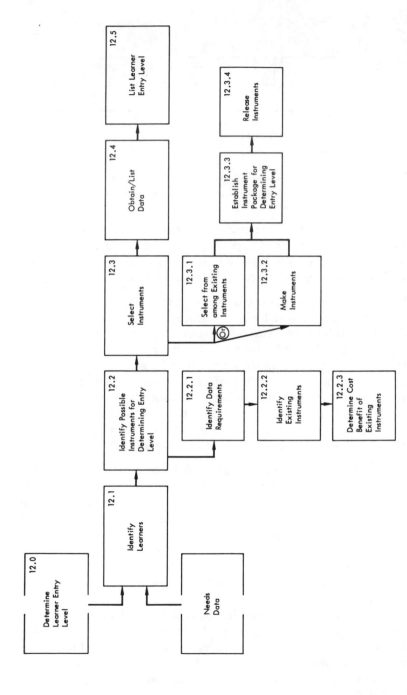

Figure 5.15. A partial function analysis dealing with individualization of instruction. Note that function 12.0 is shown as an "open" (or reference) block, indicating that there is more of this analysis located elsewhere.

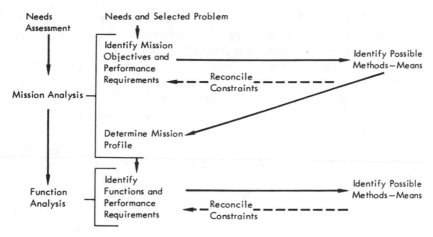

Figure 5.16. Diagrammatic relationship between mission analysis, function analysis, and methods-means analysis.

It should also be noted that in function analysis, as in all of the other system analysis phases, only "what" is to be done is indicated, not "how" to get it accomplished.

function analysis summary and review

Function analysis is the process of breaking each function into its component parts while also identifying interactions. Function analysis really commences during the mission analysis when the mission profile is derived. The mission profile is also known as the top level of function analysis. Function analysis continues, layer-by-layer (Figure 5.14), until the resulting functions are no longer clusters of products but are single units of performance. These single units of performance are arbitrarily called "tasks." Therefore, function analysis usually has several levels of break-outs until task analysis is reached. Task analysis is covered as a system analysis option later.

Function analysis formally proceeds from the analysis of the functions identified in the mission profile. These functions come from the mission profile and may be called subfunctions, since they do derive from higher level (or top) functions. Function analysis deals with products—those individual accomplishments which must be delivered in order to meet the mission objective (and thus reduce or eliminate the need from which the mission objective was derived).

Function analysis continues until all the functions have been analyzed and identified for all the top-level (mission profile) functions. This tells <u>what</u> must be accomplished to achieve each top-level function. All the functions, subfunctions, and so on are revealed until vertical expansion of the mission profile is complete. Then all the functions describing <u>what</u> has to be done to meet the mission objective and its performance requirements are identified.

Each time a function is identified, performance requirements for it must be specified. That is, one must identify in precise, measurable terms what must be delivered or completed to accomplish a given function. This performance requirement identification for each function resembles that which is accomplished in identifying the performance requirements for the mission, except that it occurs at each lower-level function that is analyzed and named. There is a continuous process of determining <u>what</u> must be completed, as well as the criteria for accomplishment and the kinds of lower-order products that constitute the function.

The differences among analyses at the various levels are a matter of degree rather than kind; there really is no difference in approach or tools used for a mission analysis, mission profile and the function analysis of any one of its functions. That is, the process is exactly the same, only the actual functions differ. Miniature or subordinate "missions" are identified each time a function is "broken out." Performance requirements must be set for each function even if it is the very first one—performance requirements of the mission—or the very last function that can be broken out.

In function analysis, as in mission analysis, the planner's job is to identify the major milestones for achieving a function and to identify the criteria (the performance requirements) by which to know when a function has been successfully performed or completed.

function analysis and feasibility

A Preview of Methods-Means Analysis

Each time a function (or a family of functions) and its associated performance requirements are identified, it becomes necessary to check in order to see if one or more possible methods-means exist for achieving those requirements. (This subject is further detailed in Chapter 6 on methods-means analysis.)

There is a requirement for constant checking back through previous steps and data and to the original needs statement to assure that the final identification of "whats" will be internally consistent and have external validity. That is, it must be determined that all the functions are compatible with one another as well as with the need, the problem, and other functions at all levels. Figure 5.16 summarizes both mission analysis and function analysis.

If there is one or more possible methods-means, then we may continue the function analysis to the next level. However, if there is not at least one possible methods-means, we have a constraint that must be reconciled before proceeding to the next level. (A restraint, in distinction, is any specification or condition, such as budget level, or values of partners. Without attempting to find a methods-means, one cannot say with certainty that a constraint exists. A restraint, actually, is a type of performance requirement, and thus provides a challenge to meet it or revise as required.)

Deciding When to Stop Doing a System Analysis

One does a system analysis only to the extent required to answer important questions. If the question relates to strategic planning, the mission objective, and mission profile along with the performance requirements might suffice. If wanting to determine curriculum objectives, then specifying to one, two, or more levels of function analysis may be necessary.

In some instances, the planner might want to provide further guidance on specific course content, courses, programs, projects, or particular characteristics which will allow for the design and development of actual interventions. In this instance, further detail of the actual tasks composing the lower level functions may be important. When this level of detail and specificity is desired, another system analysis step (and product) is required: the identification of job tasks. (Job tasks should not to be confused with a learning task analysis [Gagne, 1985] which identifies the learning steps involved in accomplishing a job task.)

task analysis: a system analysis option

"Tasks" may be defined as units of performance which, when collected, constitute a function. Thus task listing and description (here collectively called task analysis) form a possible final "breaking-down" step in system analysis. Task analysis flows from the lowest level of function identified before "units of performance" are identified.

The difference between mission, function, and task analysis is a difference of degree rather than of kind. Using the previous analogy of a microscope, we recall that each time a function is examined under a greater degree of magnification, more detail is visible; a task, then, is the lowest level of detail in a system analysis. It is the lowest level of analysis that will indicate <u>what</u> must be done to get a higher-order function accomplished. (Another analogy may be considered: a bead is to a necklace as a task is to a function.)

Tasks may be derived from the total ongoing system analysis process, where (1) an overall product, output, or outcome was identified in the mission objective and its performance requirements, (2) the basic functions required to accomplish the mission were identified (the mission profile), and (3) each of these basic (or top-level) functions was analyzed to determine the requisite lower-order products (or subfunctions). Finally, each identified function and subfunction may be broken down into single facets, or units of performance, and these may be listed and analyzed to determine the final, lowest level of performance requirements to accomplish each. The relation of task analysis to mission analysis and function analysis is shown in Figure 5.17.

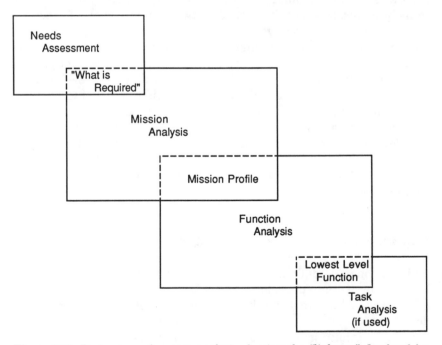

Figure 5.17. Basic steps of system analysis showing the "linkages" (bordered by broken lines), or overlapping aspects, which relate the various levels.

When the detailed analysis is at the task level and all the performance requirements are identified for each of the tasks, the planner has, for the first time, determined all the "whats" for successful problem solution. Task analysis then provides the complete array of "what is to be done" down to the level of understanding actual requirements for implementation of the plan.

The Two Basic Steps of Task Analysis

Task analysis may be conceived of as occurring in two basic steps:

(1) Identifying the basic tasks (or steps) involved in accomplishing an overall function

(2) Determining the characteristics of the tasks, their performance requirements, and their context, and putting these in a time-ordered sequence

Some authors (cf. Mager and Beach, 1967; Mager, 1988) use the nomenclature of "task listing" and "task detailing." The task steps are listed, and then such things as type of performance and learning difficulty are determined as part of the task-detailing process. Any useful task analysis should include a comparable two-step process. Here the two steps are called task listing and task description.

Task-listing, of course, consists of the identification of the basic subelements or steps involved in accomplishing an overall function and delivering a required product. Task description is the determination of the characteristics of each of the tasks or steps, including the context and performance requirements for accomplishment and the time relationships and criticality of each.

TASK LISTING

The listing of the tasks (or units of performance) that constitute a given function can be thought of as a checklist; a sequential listing of tasks that, taken together, will yield the overall function from which they derive. An example of a task listing might be a hypothetical checklist for test construction using item analysis as a part of the test construction process. Refining this hypothetical example, one might conceive of an overall mission that would require a currently non-existing vehicle—such as a test for identifying learner skills, knowledges, attitudes, values, and abilities—for predicting successful performance in music school. There would be, then, a mission objective, performance requirement, a mission profile, function analysis (including additional associated performance requirements), and finally a lower level function indicating the requirement to complete an item analysis for a hypothetical test. The hypothetical "checklist" or task listing might be something like the following:

(1) List the test item numbers.

(2) Mark another column as test alternatives a̲, b̲, c̲, and d̲.

(3) Enter on the summary sheet, for each test and for each item, the incorrect alternatives selected for each item.

(4) Sum up the incorrect alternatives selected for each item and for each possible alternative (a̲, b̲, and d̲).

(5) Identify the ten most frequently missed test items by summing across alternatives missed for each test item.

(6) Identify the frequency of the missed alternatives selected for each test item in the "top ten."

(7) Prepare a summary listing of the data collected for the item analysis for this test.

It should be noted that the listing avoids determining how the tasks are to be performed: for example, it does not indicate that any could or should be done by a computer, although the possibility exists. The purpose of the task listing is merely to identify the tasks to be accomplished, regardless of who or what is to become involved. In actuality, tasks could be accomplished by people, equipment, or people and equipment. It is not the purpose of a task analysis or a task listing to identify how a task will be performed, but only to name the tasks and the order they are to be performed.

In this initial listing (or checklist phase) other data may be collected. For instance, Mager and Beach (1967) suggest the determination of "frequency of performance," "importance," and "learning difficulty" for each of the tasks identified. This procedure would seem to be especially useful when one is designing curriculum, or a training program per se. However, for most educational planning requirements, the simple listing of task components provides sufficient information for most task analyses.

If it is decided that the definition of "what is to be done" is complete enough after the accomplishment of task listing, then, as with the other steps of system analysis, the analyst should list on a separate sheet the performance requirements associated with each task. The task analysis is completed when the performance requirements or task descriptions have been determined.

TASK DESCRIPTION[19]

After the task listing has been completed, the next step is (or could be) to determine the salient characteristics of the tasks involved. For instance, there might be such important considerations as the environment in which a task or series of tasks is to be performed, physical requirements, health and safety requirements, nature of the stimulus that signals that the task should begin, the nature and type of response that is required, the time requirements for the beginning and ending of a task, and the order and relationship between the tasks and/or subtasks.

For this reason, the task description generally takes the information from the task listing, arranges it on a time-based scale, and identifies the outstanding characteristics of the task and the context in which it is to be accomplished. As an example for a generic task analysis, the following items might require detailed specification in the task description phase, and the completion of the task analysis would oblige the system analyst (or planner) to provide these data (or more). Such a tentative list to consider in the task description phase would be:

(1) Stimulus characteristics that "signal" the requirement to begin or start

(2) Response characteristics of the required response, including whether it requires a binary (yes-no or on-off) choice, a simple manipulation, a discrimination, a complex hand-eye or psychomotor coordination, or no response at all

(3) Force or energy requirements

(4) Physiological, medical, legal, or health considerations (if people might be involved)

(5) Location for task, such as indoors, outdoors, in snow, at designed workspace, or in any number of a variety of locations

(6) Tools, devices, or instruments that are necessarily involved in the performance of the task

(7) Other data inputs required for the successful completion of the task

(8) Time requirements

(9) Criticality of the task—would the total mission be destroyed if this task were not accomplished correctly the first time, or could it be redone if performed incorrectly or out of sequence?

[19]Task description may be especially useful in system design and development, after the methods-means have been selected and further definition of the selected methods-means (for instance, a video disc-based instructional sequence) is required.

By and large, task description charts are prepared for this phase of task analysis. Many and varied task analysis formats may be used, and selection depends on the required results of the analysis. Such formats vary from a basic and simple one suggested by Mager and Beach (1967), which utilizes four columns: (1) task number, (2) steps in performing the task, (3) type of performance, and (4) learning difficulty—to quite complex man-machine interaction formats used in the aerospace field, which might include detailed physiological and psychological considerations and relationships.

The steps for performing such a task description are as follows:

Step 1—List all the tasks and subtasks necessary to accomplish the function being analyzed. This is the same derivation process employed in the break-out of the mission profile and the function analysis. The tasks identified are placed in sequence, the order in which they will occur. In identifying the tasks, we want to make them independent, so there will be no (or minimal) overlap. This is the task-listing process.

Step 2—List, by tasks, the stimulus requirements (if relevant). These are the "input" requirements, the data required by the "operator" (or "doer" of the task when it is assigned) to perform the tasks. State what form the data will or must be in to be usable.

Step 3—List the response requirements (the action requirements). These are the operations, the number of times each will occur, and the time necessary to perform the operation, if time is a real consideration.

Step 4—By task, list the support requirements. These are the kinds of materials and equipment necessary to support the operation of the task and the types of personnel or equipment required as "operators."

Step 5—List the performance criteria. Here is the specification of the product of the task. Just as a mission will produce a product, and a function will produce a product (or subproduct), so will a task produce a product—a performance result. The performance requirements of the product of the task may be such items as: (1) eliminate errors, (2) list must contain all items, (3) copy must be nonsmudged and readable, and (4) form must have adequate space for teacher notations.

Step 6—Specify the prerequisite knowledge and/or skills the operator must have in order to be able to perform a given task. If, for example, in the preparation of proposal there is a necessity for a high skill level of art work, then advanced art capability may be a critical requirement and as such is a prerequisite that must be noted.

Table 5.1 presents a hypothetical task description for an administrative function. It represents an arbitrary selection of a task-analysis format.

As a matter of practice, the lowest-level subfunction that is being analyzed at the task level is always identified by the function number from which it derives. This function number (e.g., 4.1.1) is usually placed in the upper left-hand corner of the task analysis form. Failure to identify the function being analyzed will serve to confuse just about everyone.

The task analysis format selected by the planner should be only as complex as is necessary to supply the data required in the planning process itself. The important thing to remember and include in the task description is that it must specify the total requirements for accomplishing the task. Remember that the purpose of performing a system analysis is to identify the requirements for the accomplishment of a given mission. The system analysis process indicates all the parts and the relations between the parts for accomplishing a given mission.

Thus system analysis reveals, in layers, the subsystems involved in mission accomplishment and the requirements for performing each. A task analysis should include the performance requirements for each task or task element in order to provide the detailed information and criteria that would further assure that the analysis product will reveal the most relevant and practical possibilities (methods and means) for accomplishing the function being task-analyzed. The results of a task analysis are useful in system design and development, especially having a direct input into learning specifications as well as to network-based techniques for management and control (see Chapter 7 for further detail concerning the relation between such tools as PERT and a system approach).

task analysis summary

Task analysis, when used, is the "lowest level" of a system analysis; it derives from a mission analysis and the related function analysis and thus provides the final level of detail required to identify all the "whats" for problem solution.

TABLE 5.1 An example of an administrative Task Analysis.

Subfunction 4.1.1							Administrative Tasks			
	Input (Stimulus) Requirements		Response (Action) Requirements				Support Requirements		Performance Criteria	Prerequisite Knowledge or Skill Requirement
Task (in performance or "doing" terms)	Data	Form	Operation	No.	Time	Materials	Equipment	Personnel		
Obtain list of items	Items from 2.0		Physically pick up	1				Clerk	None	None
Sequence Items	Items on last cumulative folder sequence		Note relevant cumulative sequence			Paper, pencil,		Clerk	Include all items, sequence follows	None
			List items in order	1					cumulative sequence	
Design format	Sequence of items		Locate name column	1		Paper, pencil,		Draftsman	Space for all items	Elementary drafting skill
			Count items	1						
			Measure paper						Adequate notation space in each column	

(continued)

TABLE 5.1 (continued).

	Subfunction 4.1.1							Administrative Tasks			
Task (in performance or "doing" terms)	Input (Stimulus) Requirements		Response (Action) Requirements				Support Requirements		Performance Criteria	Prerequisite Knowledge or Skill Requirement
	Data	Form	Operation	No.	Time	Materials	Equipment	Personnel		
			Divide space available by items	1						
			Locate items columns							
Prepare Reproducible	Data form with items		Select Reproducible, adjust, and align	1 1		Stencil correction fluid, ruler, stylus	Typewriter	Typist	No errors	Knowledge of stencil preparation
			Prepare Rule columns	1						
Reproduce data form	Reproducible		Obtain paper	1		Paper	Offset	Pressman	Readable, non-smudged copy	Skill in operation of offset press
Store on shelf			Run press	1						

Task analysis consists of two subparts, that relating to the identification and ordering of the steps to be taken (task listing) and that which identifies the salient characteristics and requirements of successful task accomplishment (task description). Together, these two parts constitute a task analysis that tells what units of performance are to be accomplished and the performance requirements associated with each task. Frequently, the task listing along with its performance requirements will suffice for the task analysis.

The format for conducting and reporting a task analysis is not firm or fixed. The format should be designed (or selected) to ensure that the relevant data for planning decision making are provided to the system planner. It is critical that any format utilized provide data on the nature of the task and the performance requirements (specifications) for the successful completion of each task.

The difference between mission analysis, function analysis, and task analysis is a difference of degree rather than of kind. The task analysis is a small-scale version of a function analysis—it is an identification and breaking down of the elements required to accomplish something. In task analysis, however, more detailed performance information is obtained and reported. This will provide, by and large, the basic structure and information for the actual design, implementation, test, and evaluation of the educational plan when put into operation.

Task Analysis, Function Analysis, Mission Analysis, and Their Relationship

The three system analysis tools we have considered so far are all concerned with determining "what" is to be accomplished to get us, effectively and efficiently, from where we are to meeting the identified and selected needs. The analysis proceeds in layers, or levels, to determine all the requirements for successful problem solution by identifying all the aspects of the problem and setting detailed specifications for the resolution of the problem.

Performance requirements—As with the preceding steps of mission analysis and function analysis, task analysis requires the determination of measurable specifications—performance requirements. In the task analysis process, however, the determination of these specifications is formalized in the task analysis format that is actually selected.

At the function analysis stage (as well as in task analysis, if we do one), we may perform an ongoing feasibility study by determining, at each stage of analysis, if there are any methods and means (tactics and tools) to accomplish the functions (or tasks) and their associated performance requirements.

Because task analysis, when employed, is the final "breaking-down" step in system analysis, the final feasibility analysis is completed after tasks and their specifications have been delineated. Figure 5.17 showed the relationship among mission, function, task, and methods-means analyses.

Mission, function (and task analyses); deciding on levels—The difference between mission, function, and task analysis is arbitrary and depends on one's starting place. One possible way of knowing when you have reached the task level is to ask yourself "if I break it down any further, would I have to start stating 'how' the job would have to be done?" If the answer would be "yes," stop, you are at the task level. An analysis should be carried down only to the level necessary for the analyst to be reasonably assured that he will "get back" the necessary information required for decision making.

glossary

Function   one of a group of related results (or products or subproducts) contributing to a larger result. Together they form a mission profile, which if accomplished will achieve a mission.

Function flow block diagram   the diagrammatic representation of functions that show the order and relations among functions. The forward order is shown by the numbers and the solid lines with arrows, while revision pathways are shown with broken lines, also with arrows. The functions are, in actuality, products.

Parallel functions   functions that can occur simultaneously or in the absence of a required order of accomplishment.

Series functions   functions related to one another in linear and dependent fashion. An example might be wiring of Christmas tree lights.

Task   units of peformance which, when collected, constitute a function.

Task analysis   the "lowest level" of a system analysis; it derives from a mission analysis and the related function analysis and thus provides the final level of detail required to identify all the "whats" for problem solution.

exercises

1. Given a mission objective, performance requirements, and mission profile as developed in the exercise in Chapter 4, perform a function analysis adhering to the five rules of function analysis and maintaining functional levels. The final product of the function analysis will be in the

form of a function flow block diagram and will have the following characteristics:

    a. All functions derived are in a logical sequence.
    b. All blocks are square or rectangular.
    c. All blocks contain an appropriate number.
    d. All blocks are connected with solid lines.
    e. All feedback functions are designated by broken lines.
    f. All functions in series sequence are shown in horizontal sequence.
    g. All parallel sequences are shown in vertical sequence.
    h. All numbers are by function level and identified according to the
       "parent" higher-level function, following a decimal pattern.
    i. All alternate functions are designated by an "OR" gate enclosed in a
       circle.
    j. No function is broken out into only one subfunction.
    k. Each function derived contains at least one action verb.
    l. All subfunctions derived provide for the accomplishment of the
       "parent" higher-level function.
   m. All interactions or reference functions are shown as "open" boxes.

2. For each item on the left, place the letter corresponding to the item's use
in <u>connecting</u> functions in flow block diagramming (as named on the right)
in the appropriate blank.

_____ vertical lines	a. interaction or reference function
_____ broken lines	b. alternate sequence
_____ diagonal lines	c. parallel functions
_____ horizontal lines	d. series sequence
_____ "open" box	e. feedback loop (path)

3. How many function(s) must all functions break into?

4. The purpose of function analysis is to _____
_____ , and _____
what has to be done in order to accomplish the mission objective.

5. Mission analysis and function analysis are similar in that they both are
concerned about _____ be ac-
complished.

6. In the following functions below, specify whether the function is "higher
level" (H) or "lower level" (L) relative to each other in this group:

    a. Obtain Ph.D.
    b. Identify required comprehensive exam topics.
    c. Select topic for term paper.
    d. Identify instruction criteria.
    e. Identify comprehensive examination preparation courses.
    f. Pass comprehensive exams.

7. In a function flow block diagram, a broken line indicates _____
_____ .

8. In performing a function analysis, the analyst attends to _____
_____ levels of analysis at a time.

9. In referencing to a higher-order function or to another function at the same level, the box is left _____.

10. The numbering system used in the function analysis is done in a _____ fashion.

Answer (briefly) the following questions:

11. What is the role of the function analysis?

12. How does the function analysis relate to the mission analysis?

13. What part does "check—recheck—revise" play in a function analysis?

14. When an analyst has completed a function analysis, what does he have?

15. State the five rules for making a function flow block diagram.

True and False

16. Functions found in the mission profile are called first-level functions. _____

17. Breaking-out a function identifies subordinate "mini"-missions. _____

18. Each function has performance requirements. _____

19. Interactions are not shown on a function flow block diagram. _____

20. Each function must be identifiable as discrete. _____

Fill in the blanks

21. A mission objective is identified in a function flow block diagram as the number _____.

22. Open blocks are also known as _____ blocks.

23. Each block must be _____ in shape.

24. Give an example of the numbering system in function flow block diagrams: _____

25. In one sentence, define a function: _____
_____

26. In one sentence, define the function of an "OR" gate: _____
_____

27. Open blocks indicate which of the following functions?
 a. Input
 b. Feedback
 c. Output
 d. Parallel functions

28. In performing a function analysis, the analyst is identifying the _____ and not the _____
_____.

29. When performing a function analysis, the system analyst attempts:
 a. To break one function out all the way down to the task level
 b. To focus on one level of function analysis until those of equal magnitude have been identified
 c. To identify all tasks to be done

30. The top level of a function analysis is called the _____

_____ .

31. In order to begin a function analysis, the analyst requires the following three things:

    a. _____

    b. _____

    c. _____

32. If two or more functions are or can be performed simultaneously, they are said to be in _____ sequence.

33. Functions that must be performed one after the other are said to be in _____ sequence.

34. Take one of the mission profiles presented in Chapter 4, perform a function analysis on it, and produce a function flow block diagram. Take the analysis down through at least the second level of analysis.

35. For one second-level function, continue the function analysis down through the lowest product identification level. (This is called a "single-thread analysis.") Each function identified must have performance requirements—use the additional performance requirements form on page 100.

36. Given a function analysis derived above, perform a task analysis. The task analysis form will be generated by the analyst and will be related to the particular function(s) being analyzed. The task analysis will have the following characteristics:

    a. All tasks identified will be listed in sequential order.

    b. All performance requirements of each task will be listed.

    c. Any necessary stimulus to perform the task will be listed.

    d. Support requirements will be listed.

    e. Prerequisite knowledges and skills will be listed, if appropriate to the performance of the task.

37. A task analysis begins with the completion of the _____

_____ .

38. A task analysis may be considered as having two components. These are, in order, (1) _____ and (2) _____

_____ .

39. Each task analysis will differ according to the requirements of the _____ being analyzed.

40. How does task analysis relate to the previous areas developed: mission analysis, mission profile, and function analysis?

methods-means analysis

MISSION AND FUNCTION analyses (and task analysis if used) are tools with which a planner identifies and documents products to be completed in order to ensure the successful accomplishment of a mission objective. Once products have been identified, it is necessary to ascertain whether there exists, or could exist, one or more methods and means by which they may be accomplished. The system planner not only wants to identify what has to be completed and in what order, but also wants to be able to select the best possible ways and means.

In order to provide the educational system designer with the information necessary to make the best selection of ways and means (processes) to do each function, a listing of optional tactics and delivery methods (vehicles), along with the advantages and disadvantages of each, is compiled. This compilation serves as a data bank from which the system implementer will be able to later make a rational selection. The process by which the data bank is produced is called methods-means analysis.

what is a methods-means analysis?

"Methods" include the tactics for achieving detailed functions and associated performance requirements. A "means" is a vehicle by which a tactic may be achieved.

If we are facing a curriculum problem in (for example) reading, information from a system analysis would provide performance requirements for measuring when we would reach final success. From these performance requirements it would be possible to identify: (1) requirements for mastery of content; (2) demonstrable skills, attitudes, abilities, and knowledges; (3) characteristics of the population for which the behavior change program is to be designed; (4) the required nature of the context and environment in which the program is to be conducted; and (5) the environment and context in which any resulting performance would be applied. In short, we would have a data base for determining the possible techniques and tools (or methods and means) for achieving the performance requirements. A possible method for achieving these hypothetical performance requirements in reading could be "individualized instruction," which would be responsive to each individual learner's backgrounds and entry skills. A possible vehicle for implementing these methods might be programmed self-instructional materials, using a responsive device such as a video disc to enable the program to branch to remedial and additional materials, as the student's responses dictated relative to the predetermined performance requirements. Another possible methods-means combination might be a tutor in a reading laboratory utilizing tachistoscopes, tapes, and special reading materials. Still other methods-means combinations might meet the performance requirements. A methods-means analysis identifies the possible tactics and vehicles for meeting performance requirements for the functions, and lists the advantages and disadvantages of each.

If we were concerned with a larger focus, such as the self-sufficiency of immigrant adults, then the system analysis would provide the measurable criteria for the accomplishment of that outcome. Given such a larger frame of concern, a possible set of methods-means might include literacy training and vocational/job training.

The size of a selected educational problem area is not important . . . sooner or later, detailed requirements and alternative methods and means will be identified and considered.

The methods-means analysis does not select how the requirement will be met, it only uncovers the possible ways for achieving the performance requirements. The "how" selection is made during system design and development and is not here considered part of planning using system analysis.

Part of the methods-means analysis involves identifying the advantages and disadvantages of each option. Some tools and techniques for the selection of solutions from among the options are provided in Chapter 7.

Constraints

If a performance requirement is achievable by one or a combination of methods-means, further system analysis continues. If not,

then there exists a constraint that must be reconciled before we continue. The operational removal (or reconciliation) of a constraint
may be accomplished only by: (1) changing the performance requirement; (2) finding a possible methods-means to achieve the performance requirement; (3) redefining the limits within which the performance requirement(s) may be met, or, if none of these is possible,
(4) stopping the activity then and there.

When Is the Methods-Means Analysis Begun?

In the system analysis process, the methods-means analysis best
begins as soon as performance requirements for a product, output,
or outcome has been identified. Ordinarily this is done immediately
after the setting of one or more of the performance requirements for
the overall mission. Once the final result has been identified, the
next action is to find out if there are any possible tactics and vehicles
for accomplishing the requirements. This may be viewed as an identification of the requirements for "product" which, in turn, is
matched against the requirements for "process" to achieve the product. The methods-means may already exist, or it might be something
that is in development and will be ready at a future time or, perhaps
something that has to be "invented" and is "inventable."

A methods-means analysis may begin whenever the analyst
chooses. The experienced planner will undoubtedly find greater utility in starting the methods-means analysis as soon as a mission
objective and associated performance requirements have been identified and stated. Thus, continual identification of possible "hows,"
and the relative advantages and disadvantages of each, means that
an ongoing feasibility study is being conducted (see Figure 6.1). As
the system analysis continues, the methods-means analysis portion
coincides with it, and there is continuous checking and assurance
that it is reasonable to suppose that mission can be accomplished.

When the planner has completed the lowest level of function analysis (or task analysis, if used) and the final methods-means analysis,
there are two products:

- a data base of feasible "whats" for problem solution
- a data base of possible "hows" and the advantages and disadvantages of each

The relation between a mission, function (and task) analysis and
methods-means analysis appears in Figure 6.2, which indicates that
the methods-means analysis is "parallel" to the determination of the
mission, the functions, and the tasks on an ongoing basis.

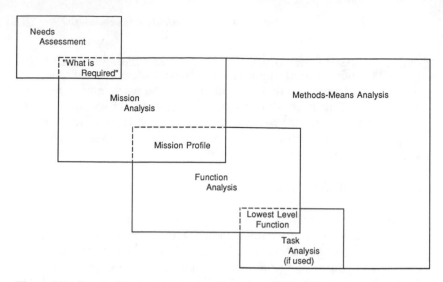

Figure 6.1. As mission, function, and task analyses (if used) continue, there may be a parallel methods-means analysis. Each time a performance requirement (or family of performance requirements) is identified, possible methods-means may also be identified.

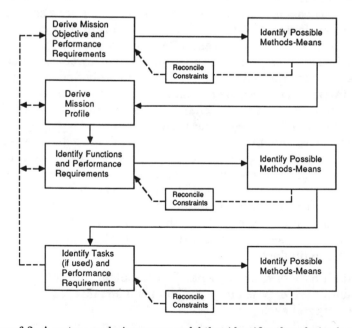

Figure 6.2. A system analysis process model that identifies the relation between the various steps in the process. Note that a continuous feasibility check is made during the process by identifying requirements in the mission and function (and task analyses, if used) and determining if there are any methods-means available for accomplishing each performance requirement or family of performance requirements.

AN OPTION

In conducting a system analysis, the methods-means analysis <u>may</u> be conducted <u>after</u> all the functions and tasks have been identified and the performance requirements for each have been determined and listed. Choosing this option may have several advantages. First, there is little (or perhaps less) distraction from the identification of "what is to be accomplished" and less risk of the possible distraction of selecting or even identifying how each performance requirement is to be done. This is to say that often a planning team, "forgetting" that the methods-means analysis does <u>not</u> select the methods-means for achieving the performance requirements, "cheats" the process by prematurely selecting the "how." To avoid this risk, or to avoid the problem of possibly mixing "whats" and "hows," the methods-means analysis may be delayed until all functions (and tasks) and performance requirements have been identified.

Figure 6.3 provides a process diagram for performing a methods-means analysis when delaying that until after all functions and performance requirements have been identified.

Another possible reason for delaying methods-means analysis is for purposes of teaching new planner/analysts the skills of system analysis. Newcomers to system analysis almost always want to "jump into" the selection of methods and means before requirements have been identified. Frequently it is easier to keep a new system analyst's attention on identifying "what" by doing the mission, function, and task analyses first, and identifying the possible "hows" last.

Actually the determination of feasibility by completing a methods-

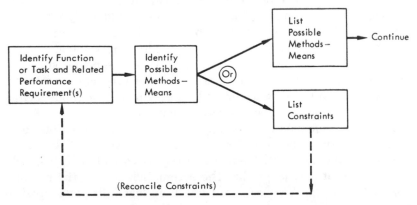

Figure 6.3. A process for performing methods-means analysis during system analysis.

means analysis after the identification of each performance requirement or a related group of performance requirements (a family of performance requirements) is generally best. The continuous attesting to feasibility may save considerable time and labor, especially if a nonreconcilable constraint is identified and system planning is drastically changed or stopped.

From What Source Does Methods-Means Information Come?

Methods-means information is found wherever valid data may be obtained. A number of texts and journals, especially those from educational technology, discuss "means" at great length and in great detail, primarily for instructional problems. Concerning other methods-means, one might well consult specialists, vendors, literature in education, and literature in other fields. This area of identification of appropriate tools and strategies is the chance to "brainstorm." Here we are not fettered by "the way it's always been done," and we may explore ideas that might superficially seem extreme so as to determine if a vehicle and/or a tactic might be usable and possibly practical to meet the performance requirements. Finally, we list all the possible methods-means for each requirement.

Must a Methods-Means Analysis be Done for Each Function (and Each Task)?

Ideally, each performance requirement should be matched with possible methods-means. In fact, each and every requirement must be met. Often, performance requirements are related in "families" – they are related and may be lumped together for identifying appropriate methods and means. Although each performance requirement must be met, the frequency of accomplishing the methods-means analysis depends on the analyst. Final methods-means possibilities can be determined only at the lowest level of function (or if done, task) analysis, and all preceding identifications of methods-means consist of progressively precise determination.

The methods-means analysis may be done for each function, for a group of functions, or even for an entire analysis level. However, remember that the methods-means analysis will identify possible constraints that may jeopardize the accomplishment of the mission in whole or in part. This constant check on feasibility is central to the validity of the system analysis and, therefore, to the successful completion of the mission. Don't try to fool yourself or the analysis!

How Are the Methods-Means Data Compiled and Stored?

In a function flow block diagram, each function is associated with a function block. Thus 0.0 would be for the mission, 1.0 would be the first function in the mission profile, 1.2 would be a derivative function from block 1.0, and so on. For each function, the analyst must record the function flow block diagram number, and with each list he or she must list the performance requirements for the particular function on a methods-means form (see Table 6.1). The planner should designate these performance requirements by letter (e.g., 1.1-A, 1.1-B, or 3.1-A). For each alphanumerically identified performance requirement, it is necessary to list next to it the methods and means that could be used to meet the requirement. These data will build up for each functional unit as the analysis continues. This record-keeping will ultimately result in a compendium of possible methods and means combinations for each performance requirement (or performance requirement family) for each function. Table 6.1 gives a sample listing and a suggested format for recording the methods-means analysis.

Must the System Analyst Summarize the Methods-Means Analysis?

After completing the system analysis, identifying performance requirements at each level, identifying possible methods-means solution vehicles for each, the analyst next prepares a methods-means summary to be used during the system design, development, and implementation phases.

To make the summary, it is necessary to arrange performance requirements and the associated methods-means possibilities into functional families. Such families are related by the top-level function from which they derive and by subfunctions (derivative functions) that may be traced to the top-level functions. This methods-means summary provides the data base of performance requirements and associated possible methods and means for use in later selection of the methods and means.

How Are Methods-Means Identified: Enter Creativity and Rationality

Do possible methods-means have to be in existence, or can they be identified so that we can "invent" new methods and/or means or synthesize old ones into new combinations? The goal is to accomplish the mission with the greatest efficiency and effectiveness. If a method or a means does not exist and it seems probable that one

TABLE 6.1 Sample methods-means identification form.

Function	Performance Requirements	Methods-Means Possibilities	Advantages	Disadvantages
8.3.1	8.3.1A Must provide signal return within 10 seconds	8.3.1A Ajax Model F	Available now	Not transportable
		8.3.1A Apex Model 10	Costs under $1,500	Reliability is .93
		8.3.1A Contract for a special purpose device	Simple to use	Costs $2,700
			Reliability of .997	Ready spring 1988
			Portable	Development and design cost of $10,800
	8.3.1B Current school office staff must be able to use (after reading an instruction booklet) not to exceed ten pages so there will be no more than 5 percent "down" time.	8.3.1B Same as all 8.3.1A MMS	Uses information sequenced by operation	Unit cost would reach 1,500 after 3,500 units delivered
			Reliability could be .999	
	8.3.1C Must operate within present school circuitry	8.3.1C Same as all 8.3.1A MMs	Portable	Ready next summer
			Could be used for performance requirement 8.2.8.4	

could be invented or synthesized, then take that option as a possibility.[20] Progress through creative new efforts and new things is important and can be a valuable spinoff of a system approach. Reach, therefore, for the valid new idea and new methods-means.

If a methods-means exists, then consider it for use. There is little sense in building something from scratch if it already may be obtained off the shelf and it will do the necessary work. On the other hand, never use something available which does not meet the requirements; settling for less than is necessary simply to save money or time is shortsighted.

procedure for performing methods-means analysis

In performing a methods-means analysis, the following steps are recommended:

(1) On the Methods-Means Identification form, record the function flow block diagram number of the function with which you are dealing.

(2) Under Performance Requirements, list the requirements that any methods-means combination must meet in order to be acceptable. Number these requirements alphanumerically to identify them with their appropriate functions.

(3) Under Methods-Means Possibilities, list any methods-means combination meeting the requirements in the previous list. Number these to match the requirements list.

(4) For each methods-means combination cited, list the advantages, such as availability, cost, time, reliability, transportability, and ease of use. Methods for such determinations are presented in Chapter 7.

(5) As in step 4, list all the known disadvantages for each methods-means combination cited.

(6) Keep the Methods-Means Analysis form with other associated functions. In a "large" analysis, you might require one file for each function in the mission profile.

(7) Upon completion of the methods-means analysis summarize it into functional families as they relate to top-level (mission profile) functions or as they <u>might</u> relate with other functions from different top-level functions.

[20]Sometimes an existing solution vehicle and tactic which are less efficient or desirable than the "inventable" one can serve as a safety back-up if the new solution doesn't pan out.

Confusing?

Doesn't this process of going from (1) functions and their performance requirements to (2) possible methods-means, to (3) constraints
(if there are no possible methods-means combinations) become confusing? It might seem so at first! But we are attempting to "capture"
the process of system analysis. System analysis looks at the method-
means derivation effort as a way of learning how the parts do in fact
go together. The description of what this process is and does may
sound complicated. However, another look at the process shown diagrammatically in Figure 6.2 should provide clarification.

The process of checking each function and the related performance
requirements to see if there is a possible methods-means combination is essential. It will give assurance that on completion of analysis, the product, output, or outcome will be achievable and will not
result in the selection of some end which is not achievable. Thus the
system designer can deal in realities and "achievements," not in
dreams (or broken dreams) and unfulfilled promises.

the methods-means analysis as a feasibility study

The methods-means analysis serves several crucial functions.
First, it identifies the alternative possible methods and means (or
strategies and tools) and lists the advantages and disadvantages of
each for each performance requirement or group of performance requirements. Second, when used in an ongoing fashion as described
in Figure 6.2, it constitutes a feasibility study. A third function it
serves is to force a consideration of alternatives for solving our problems, since we must list, whenever possible, at least two alternative
methods-means for each performance requirement. These three
features of a methods-means analysis deserve further discussion.

We have already noted that for each performance requirement (or
family of related performance requirements) we list on a separate
sheet the associated function number, the performance require-
ment(s) accompanying that particular function, and also the advantages and disadvantages for each identified possible methods-means
combination. This listing provides a set of basic data for making the
actual selection of methods and means at a later time.

We are conducting an ongoing feasibility study because there is a
constant determination of "what is to be done?" (the mission, function, and task analyses) and a determination of "can it be done?" (the
methods-means analysis). The identification of a constraint—lack of

a methods-means for achieving a performance requirement–signals that there is a feasibility problem. When a constraint is reconciled, feasibility has been substantiated and the analysis continues. If a constraint cannot be reconciled, then the project (or at least one part of the project) is not feasible. This ongoing feasibility study assures us that, if and when we do complete task analysis and the methods-means analysis at a given level, we can in all probability meet the identified needs. We have identified all the requirements for problem resolution and have further identified the possible strategies and tools for meeting all requirements, including the listing of feasible alternative ways of getting the jobs done.

During the system synthesis (especially step 3.0 in the generic educational problem-solving model–Figure 2.1, page 32) we are going to use the system analysis information to select the most effective and efficient methods and means for meeting the identified needs. Of great importance in this decision will be the information we have gathered during the system analysis, especially the methods-means analysis. Some methods for this are suggested in the next chapter.

Cost-Results Analyses

Included and essential in any consideration of methods and means are the factors of time and cost (cf. Levin, 1983). Of increasing usefulness in education today is a criterion which relates results with money: relating cost and product, cost and output, as well as cost and outcome. They have labels of cost-effectiveness, cost-benefit, and cost-utility (Kaufman and Stone, 1983). Cost-results analyses are another way of asking the simple questions of "What do I give?" and "What do I get?"

Cost-results analyses cannot be performed without the prior acquisition of certain data (so that the analyst may decide among the alternative methods and means identified in the methods-means analysis). When listing advantages and disadvantages, special attention should be devoted to the determination of variables and criteria that will be useful in the coming tradeoff between costs and results when the methods and means are actually selected (Chapter 7). It should be noted that cost results analyses are not the same as cost efficiency; in functional education we are focusing on benefits (outcomes, outputs, and/or products relating to documented needs), and the mere achievement of efficiency without benefits is a relatively shallow accomplishment. Thus in conducting the methods-means analysis it is particularly important to collect and list data concerning the time and cost dimensions as they relate to the performance requirements.

Requirements for Methods-Means Analysis

Creativity, innovation, and methods-means analysis should all go together. The suggestion that, for each performance requirement (or group of related performance requirements), there are at least two alternative methods-means listed, is an attempt to force the analyst to consider new and innovative possibilities. Frequently we are tempted to pick the solution vehicle with which we have the most familiarity and which has been successful in the past—an unfortunate tendency which inhibits true progress in better meeting the needs of learners. By formally considering the highest likely number of methods-means alternatives, the analyst is encouraged to be bold, innovative, and creative. Indeed, innovativeness and creativity are encouraged by a system approach.

As the final step in performing an educational system analysis, it might be remembered that this step, like all the others, is designed only to identify "what" is to be done, not to select "how" to do it. In the case of methods-means analysis we are answering the following question:

"What 'hows' are possible, and what are the advantages
and disadvantages of each?"

All of the system analysis as described here is concerned with planning educational systems. By using it, one is identifying both needs and requirements for meeting the needs; feasible alternatives for effective and efficient problem solving are also identified. The completion of the methods-means analysis signals that "what is to be done" has been accomplished; now "how to do it" may be determined, implemented, and evaluated . . . and this is the purpose of doing educational system planning.

summary

Since the methods-means analysis relates to all the other steps of a system analysis, a summary may be made diagrammatically (Figure 6.4). A process chart summarizing the steps of system analysis appears in Figure 6.4.

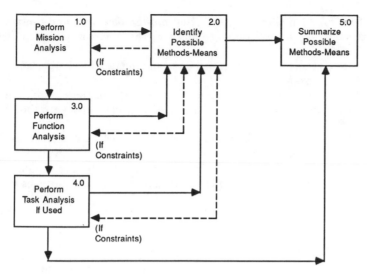

Figure 6.4. The process for performing a methods-means analysis.

glossary

Constraint   the situation where at least one methods-means combination cannot be found which will meet performance requirements. A constraint may be eliminated by changing the objective and its performance requirements (which then might not be responsive to the documented need), create a new methods-means which previously did not exist, or, finally, stop.

Cost-results analysis   an analysis relating costs of a result (product, output, and/or outcome) with the payoffs to be accrued from the successful achievement of the results. In its simplest form, cost-results analyses ask the two simultaneous questions of "What do I give?" and "What do I get?" There are tools for determining actual or predicted cost benefit, including the tools of "Planning-Programming-Budgeting System (PPBS)," and systems analysis (see Chapter 7).

Feasibility   capability of being carried out or completed successfully, with predicted success significantly greater than chance.

exercises

1. Given a representative, valid function analysis derived from one function of a mission profile dealing with an educational problem, perform a methods-means analysis meeting the criteria for methods-means analysis stated below.

For each function starting at 0.0, the mission objective, and continuing down through at least one task, conduct a methods-means analysis at each level of analysis.

    a. All functions will be identified by a function flow block diagram numbering system.

    b. All performance requirements lists will contain those requirements specific to the function being analyzed and identified with that function alphanumerically.

    c. All methods and means and possibilities cited will meet the performance requirements and will be identified alphanumerically.

    d. Each methods-means combination cited will be accompanied by specifications designating the advantages and disadvantages for its use.

2. What is a method?

3. What is a means?

4. When is the methods-means analysis begun?

5. From what source does the methods-means information come?

6. What is the product of a methods-means analysis? What data does it contain?

7. How are the methods-means combinations identified?

8. There are seven basic steps in the performance of a methods-means analysis. List them.

CHAPTER 7

doing what you've planned

BY THIS TIME you might be wondering what to do with all these organizational elements, boxes, arrows, performance requirements, and methods-means analyses. Obviously, a plan is not worthwhile unless it achieves useful results.

Needs assessment, problem solving, and system analysis, as defined in this book, are tools for planning educational systems. Their use encourages us to start from a formal determination of educational needs, and provides information for selecting the most important objectives with the highest priority for action. The discrepancy that is chosen to be acted upon then becomes the stated problem, and the mission analysis identifies the outcome specifications and a management plan (mission profile) for getting from our current results to the required ones. Function analysis (and task analysis, if we employ it) provide us with detailed information concerning what enroute results we have to deliver in order to reach each element in the mission profile. The system analysis also notes the necessary interactions and interrelations among the various functions (and tasks). Finally, the methods-means analysis provides a feasibility determination that helps us to know if: (1) objectives are realizable and (2) possible alternative strategies and tools exist for achieving each of the many requirements for problem solution.

At this point we have the answers to the following questions:

(1) What are the needs?

(2) What are the problems of highest priority?

(3) What are the requirements to meet the needs and thus solve the problem(s)?

(4) What are the possible tactics and tools to achieve the required performances, and what are the advantages and disadvantages of each?

Thus we have identified all the feasible "whats" for problem solution. Referring to the six-step process model of a system approach, we have completed the first two functions: 1.0, identify problem based on needs and 2.0, determine solution requirements and alternatives.

We would now be ready for the "synthesis" portion of a system approach, and we have the necessary information to act with assurance that we would meet the high-priority identified needs. Thus, needs identification and the system analysis portion of educational system planning (as defined here) are accomplished, and we may proceed to plan for system synthesis.

The steps and tools involved in a system approach's two phases are:

Phase	Method
Identify, document, and select needs	The OEM
Get from what is to what should be	Problem-solving process

The needs assessment and system analysis have allowed us to identify all of the requirements for meeting the needs and resolving the problems. The six-step problem solving process may be applied at each and every step or phase: it will identify and verify needs and allow us to systematically resolve them. In applying a system approach, we actually follow the six-step problem-solving process, although it might be done in six steps or many more. Following are the tools which we may apply in an implementation of a system approach:

Six-Step Problem-Solving Process	Tools
Identify problem from needs	Needs assessment and the OEM
Determine solution requirements and solution alternatives	System analysis
Select solution strategy from among alternatives	Systems analysis techniques, management and control techniques
Implement	
Determine performance effectiveness and efficiency	Summative, formative, and goal-free evaluation
Revise as required	Management and redesign techniques

The relationship between needs assessment and problem solving was depicted in Figure 2.13 which showed that each time one wishes to meet needs or to verify them and then resolve them systematically, one may apply the six-step problem-solving process.

As discussed earlier, the OEM conceptual framework is useful for identifying and selecting needs and problems. System analysis reveals the detailed requirements and identified alternative solutions. After doing these, we are now ready to select the tools, techniques, and methods required to allow the needs to be met: planning for the system synthesis. Again, this book deals only with planning: Identifying what has to be accomplished to make certain one is solving the right problems.

selecting solution strategies from among alternatives

As a result of the methods-means analysis, we know the possible methods and means for achieving each performance requirement and the relative advantages and disadvantages of each. Based on this information, the planner (or implementer) is to select the best options (function 3.0 in the generic six-step problem-solving process model). This can be a messy but rewarding job. Although not consistently labeled as such in the literature, the tool for selecting the most effective and efficient ways and means is called "systems" analysis. This is different from system analysis, but draws upon its products.

Methods-means selection is frequently (but unfortunately) made by hunches, history, and intuition, with the likelihood that the latest gimmick or the most comfortable solution will be picked. It does not have to be, however. Useful conceptual frameworks and techniques are available (cf. Cooley & Bickel, 1986; Myers, 1984; Phi Delta Kappa, 1984). Techniques for deciding among alternative solutions have been developing for several years. Such systems analysis tools as cost-benefit analysis, relevance trees, decision trees, delphi technique, cross-impact analysis, queuing theory, cycle analysis, nominal group technique, and polling are among some of the most well-known.

While this book is not about implementation and operations in education, following are capsule summaries of several of these useful tools and approaches. These are presented to let the reader know of their existence and to encourage more reading where individual situations call for synthesis-type activities.

Systems Analysis

The technique of systems analysis as defined by Cleland and King (1968) is different from the definition of system analysis as described in previous chapters. Cleland and King define this tool as:

(1) Systematic examination and comparison of those alternative actions which are related to the accomplishment of desired objectives

(2) Comparisons of alternatives on the basis of the resource cost and the benefit associated with each alternative

(3) Explicit consideration of uncertainty

Conceived in this manner, systems analysis is most useful when we have already identified objectives and requirements based on needs and are ready to locate and consider possible alternative methods and means. Thus conceived, systems analysis would be most advantageously applied after the completion of educational system planning, and when objectives have been derived from a needs assessment and system analysis. (System analysis, as used in this book, identifies what should be accomplished in the first place. Systems analysis assists in the selection of the best ways and means to meet the objectives identified and selected in system analysis.)

Systems analysis may be thought of as the generic approach to selecting solution strategies from among options. The tools and techniques which followed thus may be considered specific "systems analysis tools."

OPERATIONS RESEARCH

According to Alkin and Bruno (1970), operations research

> . . . may be considered a method of obtaining optimum solutions to problems in which relationships are specified and criteria for evaluating effectiveness are known. Operations research summarizes alternatives into mathematical expressions and models. It then identifies the set of alternatives that maximizes or minimizes the desired criterion for evaluating effectiveness.

It might be concluded, then, that operations research has potential but no utility for educational implementation until the goals, objectives, and requirements for educational accomplishment have been determined and are in a form that allows for quantification. If viable education system planning is accomplished using the tools of needs assessment and system analysis to identify and justify goals and objectives, operations research may be of significant utility.

PLANNING-PROGRAMMING-BUDGETING SYSTEM (PPBS)

Most discussions of PPBS note that as a tool, it is best used for taking the objectives of education, identifying alternative courses of action intended to meet the objectives (including a determination of costs and benefits associated with each), and ranking the various alternative choices (sometimes called "systems") in terms of their respective costs and benefits. Then choices among the alternatives may be made on a more rational basis, and it is possible to derive a budget based on cost of achieving objectives.

Planning and budgeting go together, although (sadly) the budget is often made up before the planning has been accomplished. Or put another way, the budgeting systems seem often to be more important than the planning: a serious and often fatal flaw. Many operations are weakened by being driven by dollars alone, and the objectives and needs are made to fit the money available. First should come the identified needs, then the problems, then the detailed objectives, and only then the programming and budgeting.

The utility of PPBS would seem to depend greatly on the validity of the original objectives chosen for further study and evaluation.

Other tools may also be of assistance in the selection of methods and means (and perhaps also applicable in the next system approach step of implementation): simulation and operational gaming, game theory, relevance trees, decision theory, delphi technique, cross-impact analysis, queuing, cycle analysis, and polling.

SIMULATION, OPERATIONAL GAMING, GAME THEORY, AND QUEUING

Simulation is simply building and using a model of a real or predicted event or situation. It can vary from a physical mock-up of a building or a classroom to see "how it will work" in practice to quite complex, mathematical models with multiple interacting variables.

Fortunately, the increasing availability of computers allow for simulations to be within the reach of most school agencies. Even computer programs for powerful personal computers are available for generating alternative budget/results scenarios. In the future, even more powerful simulation possibilities will exist as computers provide more memory and become smaller and less costly.

Suppose we want to know how well a school layout, selected from among our identified alternative methods-means, might work. We could build a miniature model of it and attempt to extrapolate its usefulness and problems in order to help "predict" its effectiveness and efficiency. Or suppose we have derived our detailed performance requirements based upon our defined needs and selected problems. With the input of different budget and condition parameters, the computer (and its program) may generate different results at differing funding levels.

A variation of simulation (and other types of model building), operational gaming uses human beings playing roles in a given context or situation. For instance, if we were facing a major school board meeting at which several methods for raising additional funds for the schools would be discussed, we might decide to "role-play" the situation: each person would assume the character of a board member and the meeting could be predictively "created" to determine what might happen at the actual event.

Operational gaming, and simulation, too, may be used at any time during the implementation phase. A manager might want to carry out a simulation or game before taking a specified and previously planned action to test whether it will in fact yield the desired result. By so doing, there would be the opportunity to change the approach to implementation or even revise methods and means, if necessary.

Game theory (cf. Bell and Coplans, 1976) usually has "players" who hold opposite interests but who are equally knowledgeable and informed, who have a known number of options, and are asked to complete their task in a limited time frame. In order to make it a "game" there are payoffs (but not necessarily money), differing values, and a desire to predict correctly the right course of action. Both operational gaming and game theory attempt to simulate actual, real-world happenings before the fact.

Queuing is a mathematical method (cf. von Bertalanffy, 1968) intending to optimize waiting time in a crowding situation (such as registration of students, or scheduling of athletic or academic events). The two frequent variables used are frustration and cost.

RELEVANCE TREES AND DECISION THEORY

Relevance trees are used when one can identify hierarchies or distinct levels of complexity of events, with each lower level in a "tree" (named for the continuing branching from a common trunk) increasingly more detailed, or distinctive (cf. Martino, 1983). By breaking down a series of sequential components of a system into those approaches, tasks, jobs, or actions where problems or opportunities might occur, one can identify the associated probabilities and thus identify the best pathway or alternatives to choose.

Decision theory is used to determine optimum strategies based upon probabilities for alternatives reaching a goal (cf. Rappaport, 1986). Probabilities are assigned to each of the actions/options, with each element in the branching options and predicted consequences shown in branches (such as those in relevance trees). Points where decisions must be made or where chance influences future occurrences, are also included. One may identify the risks of alternative branch pathways by computing the probabilities of reaching the goal through each action/option.

DELPHI TECHNIQUE, NOMINAL GROUP TECHNIQUE, AND POLLING

Delphi technique is a method of getting a group response without convening groups (and thus not hinging results on face-to-face group dynamics). This technique uses the judgments of experts, or panelists, in a series of questions circulated in rounds. Each round asks, usually about future events and consequences, the respondents to provide their expectations on a given topic (e.g., when will the fundamentalists' impact upon schools diminish; when will all learners have to know how to program computers). After each set of responses, the implementer reports the median response along with the ranges of responses (usually the center 50%, called the "interquartile," ranging from 25–75%), plus, when appropriate, some of the actual comments made by the panelists.

By the end of several rounds (usually three are enough) clusters of responses are formed which reflect the serial considerations of the panelists both as they respond individually, and then having the knowledge of the responses of others.

Nominal group technique is a structured problem-resolving process designed to generate ideas and produce group consensus. In most of its forms, it encourages the participation of everyone in a group, focuses concentration on a specific question, and reaches consensus through voting.

Polling, as the name connotes, is an approach which asks representative people what are their preferences or predictions. Polls are published all the time.

One possible limitation of consensus-building approaches might lie in attempting to get consensus by leveling responses towards an agreeable center point. At risk, of course, is that the group might not be correct, and an outlying (or aberrant) point of view, which might be correct, will tend to be eliminated. Agreement is not validity.

CROSS-IMPACT ANALYSIS

Since not everything in our world happens in isolation from other variables, this approach attempts to factor-in possible interaction effects. When doing a cross-impact analysis, each event is given a probability of occurrence and a time frame for happening. Prior occurrences then determine the incidence or non-incidence of future events. For example, scientific knowledge increases, but religious values and influence do so as well; increased statewide competency testing, but greater numbers of learners going to private schools; teachers' salaries increasing, student violence increasing, etc. Given these events, times, and probabilities, a cross-impact analysis looks at arrays of changes in timing possibilities, or varies each of the predicted variables so that optional possibilities may be determined (cf. Martino, 1983; Phi Delta Kappa, 1984).

This is an especially useful tool in that it does not assume the linearity of events.

CYCLE ANALYSIS

Most of us have heard of "charting the stock market" in order to determine if cycles, known and predicted ups and downs of an ongoing series of events, can help us choose properly. In education, increased interest is being paid to the possibilities offered by analyzing the cycles of educational events, or even societal events. This technique may be used in conjunction with cross-impact analyses.

summary of selection alternatives

These alternative techniques provide the educator with methods and procedures by which the most effective and efficient tactics and tools may be determined to meet the needs and requirements derived during the needs assessment and system analysis phases. They all tend to relate to the question of cost/results, which is another way of answering the two simultaneous questions of "What do I get?" and "What do I give?" Obviously, one wants to make available the best educational conditions for the least expenditure, and such tools as those just described will help to achieve that end.

implementation: doing . . . at last!

Implementation is the actual doing of what was planned, using the selected tools and tactics. Implementation includes both the making or obtaining of the actual methods, means and materials as well as using them in the educational setting. When dealing with curriculum and materials, for example, we take the requirements from our plan, and using the results of the methods-means analysis, we then make, buy or obtain any materials and approaches. We then try them out in a preliminary study (formative evaluation), and revise them as required. After this development phase, we put them to work in the operational educational environment.

Implementation is what educators do best, since we have been rewarded most of our lives for doing things. But we receive little encouragement for planning. Implementation can be managed and controlled so that required outcomes are achieved. Of significant utility in implementation is a management and control tool called PERT (Program Evaluation Review Technique) and its close relative CPM (Critical Path Method), which are time-line, sequential graphic representations of milestones or events. These network-based management tools provide the implementer with information concerning what has to be done, when it has to be done, and what happens to everything else if one element of a plan is either early or late. Cook (1966) provides excellent expositions on network-based management tools. The data from a system analysis (and especially the task analysis) have great usefulness as the primary input into PERT or CPM.

Well-developed models and approaches are available for the design of instructional systems (cf. Branson, et al., 1975; Dick & Carey, 1985; Corrigan & Corrigan, 1985; Briggs, 1977; Gagne, 1985; Gagne & Briggs, 1979; Briggs & Wager, 1981; Reigeluth (Ed.), 1983; Merrill, 1983; Mager, 1988; etc.). In general, each of these models detail some form of the already familiar six-step model applied to learning and instruction, including:

- setting objectives based upon performance requirements
- identifying alternative methods and means for meeting the requirements
- selecting the most effective and efficient media and methods
- designing and developing the learning media, materials, and methods
- revising as required (formative evaluation)
- implementing
- determining performance effectiveness and efficiency (summative evaluation)
- revising as required

determination of performance effectiveness and efficiency (evaluation)

Evaluation is reactive. It compares results with purposes (Kaufman and Thomas, 1980). In order to evaluate something, it has to exist. Evaluation comes into play any time it is desired to determine the extent to which what has been accomplished matches that which one set out to accomplish (cf. Astin and Panos, 1971; Cooley, 1971; Isaac and Michael, 1971; Popham (Ed.), 1974; Stufflebeam (in Popham), 1974; Stufflebeam, Foley, Gephart et al., 1971). (Needs assessment, on the other hand, can be proactive since it intends to find out the gaps between "what is" and "what should be ". . . with the emphasis on "should.")

How well or how poorly the needs have been met defines performance effectiveness. A number of tools are available for evaluation in addition to the relatively comfortable norm-referenced testing instruments. Criteron-referenced testing (Glaser, 1966; Popham and Husek, 1969) is useful for accomplishing the function of valid determination of results. Other tools include, but are not limited to, national assessment as a vehicle for determining what is known by representative members of our educational charges (if we want to know about the "big" picture), and a tool which is related to, but different from evaluation—the independent educational accomplishment audit (Lessinger, 1970). An educational accountability auditor determines the extent to which an agency has accomplished its objectives, using the data of expenditures of time and money much the same way a certified public accountant audits a commercial organization. Usually, evaluation at this stage of system design and development is of the summative variety and tells us about the extent to which we did or did not meet the objectives that were derived from the documented needs.

Scriven (1967, 1973) has suggested that there are three types of evaluation: formative, summative, and goal-free. Each is useful when used at the right time, in the correct manner, and applied at the right place.

Formative evaluation compares progress with objectives, and revises as required . . . before going on (cf. Dick and Carey, 1985). Although most often applied to instructional development where an instructional package is tried out during its development to determine the extent to which it is working, larger interventions may also be subjected to this type of evaluation. For instance, the six-step problem-solving process described in this book actually contains a "formative evaluation" step: the sixth one of "revise as required," since, at each step, one compares the progress with the objectives and decides to continue or revise.

Summative evaluation is more familiar to educators. At the end of any program, project, or phase (such as a school year, or semester) a comparison may be made between obtained results and previously stated objectives. From this comparison, one may continue that which has worked, and revise that which has not.

Goal-free evaluation examines the context and situation after any intervention, without using existing goals or objectives. Rather than biasing observations to specifications in a restricted context, the evaluator goes into the operational world much the way an anthropologist would, and simply finds out what is going on, what is happening, what is working, and what should be changed. Without using objectives (or at least without being armed with formal ones), the evaluator is not constrained by possibly narrow purposes, but is free to find out what is useful, and what is not.

revised as required

Revision both occurs last as well as on a continuous and ongoing basis. (On our six-step problem-solving process, it is shown as the dotted line, "revise as required," which may be taken at any one or all steps of identifying and solving problems.) Continuous evaluation relates to the concept of formative evaluation, whereby any time the interim or in-process objectives are not being met, necessary revisions may be made. This self-correctional feature is the element which assures that the needs will be eventually met. It also provides educators with the right to fail <u>and</u> the ultimate obligation to succeed—new and boldly creative things may be tried, and if these are found wanting, new and more responsive techniques may be substituted. We may fail frequently, but the most important criterion is whether we delivered the results we set out to accomplish.

A critical aspect of valid revision is the requirement that the process information be systematically and periodically reported to the decision makers so that necessary corrective action may be taken. It is also important to keep in mind that the revise-as-required step is to take place throughout system planning and implementation. Using "formative" evaluation, there is a constant check on utility and an attempt to make the system responsive. Thus the aproach is not a rigid, unyielding procedure, but rather a "people-centered," flexible process for meeting human needs.

summary

There are a number of tools that take us from the planning of successful education outcomes to their actual achievement. These tools are not covered in detail here; the several referenced resources (plus many others) for these tools will allow the planner to make the transition to "doer."

If educational system planning, including needs assessment and system analysis, is only the beginning of the educational enterprise, it is the critical step in assuring that relevant and practical solutions will be identified, selected, and applied to real problems. It also is the first step in educational accountability—being responsible for what we are charged with accomplishing. It provides the criteria for a reasonable accountability, based on at least the following elements:

(1) Documented needs

(2) A co-commitment regarding the exact nature of the expected results from the partners in education (learners, community, and educators)

(3) A shared responsibility for the results among the partners—each partner knows and agrees on each one's precise responsibility for contributing and achieving

The suggested system approach process model and its associated tools and procedures form a basic process (and a type of rational logic) for defining and achieving realistic educational responsibility and accountability. By using it, means and ends will be placed in more proper perspective, and the utilization of means will be based not upon whim or fancy, but upon its probability of meeting high priority needs.

glossary

Criterion-referenced item   a test or evaluation item referring to a specific behavior or performance ideally derived from a needs assessment and system analysis. It provides a realistic alternative to "norm-referenced" (where a person's score is compared with all others taking a particular examination) test items.

Formative evaluation   the determination of "in-process" or ongoing activities and results, including a determination of the extent to which processes and procedures are working or have worked in meeting overall objectives and requirements. It also supplies criteria for in-process changes in an operating system.

Goal-free evaluation   the process of examining an educational situation or context without predetermined purposes, and uncovering that which is effective, and that which is not.

Operational gaming   a variation of simulation usually characterized by the assumption of roles by people in a given (hypothetical) context or situation.

Operations research   a method of obtaining optimum solutions to problems in which criteria and interrelationships are well defined, usually being expressed in mathematical models.

Program Evaluation Review Technique (PERT)   one of several network-based tools for planning the implementation of an educational system. These tools, including CPM (Critical Path Method), are time-line, sequential graphic representations of milestones or events which can show the consequences of changes in implementation activities, including changes in the categories of dollars, time, and resources.

Simulation   the building and using of a model of a real or predicted event or situation.

Summative evaluation   the customary mode of educational evaluation, wherein final outcomes or results are determined and compared with the predetermined goals and/or objectives.

Systems analysis   the tools and techniques for selecting the most effective and efficient alternatives to meet specified requirements. These usually compare costs and results among alternative ways and means for doing something based on optional resource cost and benefit and a consideration of uncertainty. Differs from "system analysis" which is used to identify and justify the goals and objectives in the first place. Included in systems analysis tools, techniques and approaches are:

- relevance trees
- decision theory
- delphi technique
- cross-impact analysis
- simulation, game theory, and operational gaming
- queuing
- cycle analysis
- nominal group technique
- polling
- PPBS and CPM
- operations research

exercises

1. What will result from conducting a needs assessment and a system analysis?

2. List the steps of a system approach that are primarily concerned with "doing," or system synthesis.

3. As used in this book, what is the relation between "system analysis" and "systems analysis?"

4. Define the following terms and state where each is used in a system approach.
   a. Summative evaluation
   b. Formative evaluation
   c. Goal-free evaluation
   d. System analysis
   e. Needs assessment
   f. OEM
   g. Systems analysis

5. Why is it important that the system analysis keeps away from selecting methods and means?

6. What are five methods for systems analysis? Give examples of situations where each may be applied.

CHAPTER 8

applying the models:
the Gotham School District

ALL EDUCATIONAL SITUATIONS are different. A specific plan which is developed for one application should not be exactly copied for another use.

The following example is based upon a hypothetical school system in an urban area. It is designed to allow you to look over the shoulder of a group to see how they went about using a system approach to educational planning. Even though this is an incomplete example, it provides the concepts and procedures which may be generalized to both your educational setting as well as to other disciplines such as training and organizational development.

In addition, an 18-step process is provided to guide you in applying that which has been presented in this book.

★ ★ ★ ★ ★
GOTHAM SCHOOL DISTRICT

In a city of 169,000 people, Gotham School District has been in operation since the late 1920s. It is a centralized system with an elected school superintendent who has an Ed.D., and has been with the system since 1979. The school board is made up of elected citizens, and all of the major policy decisions are made by them. The general statement of purpose of the Board Policy is to provide "excellence in education."

Recently, the board authorized a Planning and Human Resources Development Department, brought in an open and creative planner to head it up, and asked that several administrators, a board member, and a teacher work along with the fledgling activity. They were asked to define and achieve "excellence" as well as prepare a "strategic plan."

The superintendent, having decided to support Planning and Human Resources Development (PHRD), has given a good but not abundant budget to the department, and the director of HRD wants to develop the staff so that they can improve system effectiveness and deliver on the promise of "excellence." The PHRD held an initial staff meeting where they voted to move into planning together. They scheduled an initial workshop in Needs Assessment and System Planning, with the PHRD staff, the deputy superintendent, the head of personnel, and the supervisor of management information systems in attendance.

The first thing they do is to get a briefing on the Organizational Elements Model (OEM), and after having some questions answered to their satisfaction (e.g., is this an academic process, or is it practical; have others used it and found it worthwhile; is it really too complex to use, or will we get more comfortable with it as time goes on) they make a motion and move to implement it.

The PHRD team is told that the OEM is only a framework—a template—to allow them to identify what is being currently accomplished, what should be accomplished, and a way to "keep track" of the results of all of the system analysis products. Using the OEM as a guide, or "job-aid," they decided to plan, and now have to pick the needs assessment and planning framework: middle, comprehensive, or holistic.

The PHRD team note that most of their current work and assignments fall into the organizational elements of inputs, processes and occasionally in product. They used the OEMs as a job aid in order to allow them to relate what they are now doing and accomplishing. After doing this they realized that it was important for them to try to fill in all of the elements. Their effort, after much discussion and changes, was completed.

They decided to do a "holistic," (or strategic) plan.

They reviewed this decision with the superintendent, obtained his written approval, and then reconvened to see what would come next. The PHRD staff picked up on the process quickly and noted that these were only the initial steps. They had not yet involved other partners, and had not stated both "what is" and "what should be."

So far they had accomplished:

(1) Decide to plan educational system(s) using data from a needs assessment.

(2) Select the needs assessment and planning level (middle, comprehensive, holistic/strategic).

But who should be the partners? After reviewing holistic planning concepts, they selected two administrators, four staff teachers, a senior and freshman student, a city councilwoman, a newspaper editor, the union president at the largest industry in the district, and a member of the Minority Affirmative Action Council. This group was selected in order to have a representative sample, and to be assured that any plan-

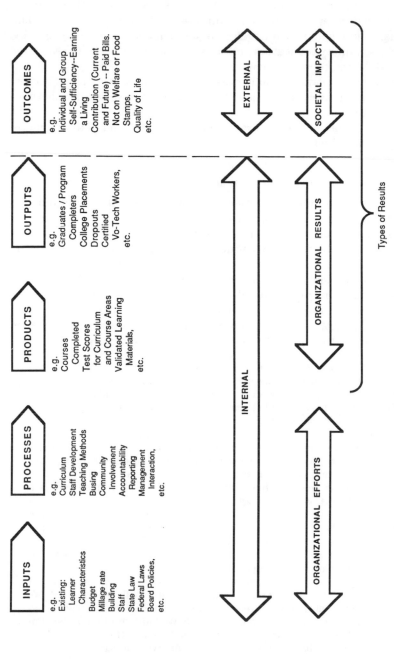

Figure 8.1. The Organizational Elements Model including some educational delivery examples of each and the relationship among the elements and the Internal and External frames of reference. Another format for these relationships is provided in Table 2.1.

ning they did would represent the various organizational and community factions and clients. The composition also better assured that the plan and results, once developed and achieved, would be seen by all the community (educators and learners, staff and citizens) as being worthwhile and representative.

The potential planning team was contacted by the PHRD Director, and they all agreed, in writing, to participate. A series of meetings were scheduled.

Thus, two more of the general needs assessment and planning steps were accomplished:

(3) Identify the needs assessment and planning partners.

(4) Obtain planning partner's participation.

In the first planning team meeting, the PHRD staff presented the concepts of Needs Assessment and System Planning, discussed the advantages and disadvantages of it, and took a vote on whether or not to use it. One member, the city councilwoman, said that she would be in favor of it, but it sounded a lot like the management-by-objective (MBO) approach she had studied in a business course. She thought that it might be dehumanizing to reduce everything to measurements. One of the teachers, the board member, and the senior student joined her in resistance. Things buzzed for about a half hour, and then the elementary teacher began speaking slowly, but very confidently:

> Your objections, it seems to me, are important and we must be certain that we do not rush to measure things just because they are easy to measure. If we captured the easy-to-measure only, we could leave out the most important part of good education, the results which are useful in today's and tomorrow's worlds.
>
> I think that we can see that if we are careful and in agreement about wanting to focus on what we accomplish and how we do it—on results and not just on procedures—we will not dehumanize and thus will not miss the important, very human and humane aspects.
>
> Education, as viewed when using this OEM model framework, is a means, a process. We should not pick our processes, or even our inputs and resources, without looking at the overall reason for this school system and all of its staff—to facilitate learning and mastery, encourage competence and school completion, to graduate contributing citizens in our community, for both today and tomorrow. To emphasize his point, he sketched the relationship, Figure 8.2, on the chalkboard.
>
> With results in focus—including measurement and objectives—and not just the procedures, we will not dehumanize and we will not trivialize. We can be accountable for both useful results and humanism, for payo⁴s and contributing to an improving quality of life. We must continue to be concerned with assisting each learner to be both self-sufficient as well as have the opportunity to have a happy, productive, and satisfying life.

A new vote was taken, and the group decided to accept the entire

Organizational Elements Model

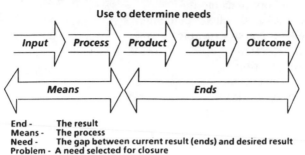

End -   The result
Means -   The process
Need -   The gap between current result (ends) and desired result
Problem - A need selected for closure

Figure 8.2.

framework. Their initial objections seem to be eliminated, at least for now.

With that, then, the next step was accomplished:

(5) Obtain planning partner's acceptance of the needs assessment and planning level (of the OEM framework).

As the elementary teacher had noted, they have only "part of the story," and they did not have any of the "what should be's," nor did they have any measurable data for any of the OEs. She suggested, and the group agreed, the next PHRD task was making the "what is" elements measurable, and moving on to the identification and documentation of the needs starting with outcomes.

They talked about possible data sources, and noted that they could collect information from school records, from U.S. census data, and from that which would be available from the state employment office. They noted that any data which were missing from the community might be obtained by using a local university student who was enrolled in the master's program in measurement and social sciences. They decided to collect data on the following:

- job placements (full or part-time)
- military acceptances
- unemployment
- welfare
- food stamps
- felony convictions
- misdemeanor convictions
- divorce
- freedom from drug and/or alcohol addiction or abuse
- commitment to mental institutions
- marriages

- community college placements
- trade school placements
- university and college placements
- college/university completions
- job satisfaction
- life satisfaction
- voter registrations
- quality of work life
- physical health level
- quality of life
- credit ratings
- home ownership
- automobile ownership
- savings
- leisure activities
- satisfaction with Gotham School District

Some of the desired data were collected within the Gotham School District, and the graduate student collected her data and reported them to the PHRD planning partnership team.

They filled out the Needs Assessment matrix with these data, which would then be used for the "outcomes" cells of the matrix. (This would also be entered into their OEM framework . . . just to keep track of everything and make certain they weren't missing important information.)

	WHAT IS	WHAT SHOULD BE
Society/ Commu- nity	63% graduation rate*	
	17% divorced within 5 years	
	29% in higher education*	
	11% saving over $1,000.00	
	9% convicted, etc.	
	43% rated "average" to "high" measured perception of "Quality Way of Life"	
	11% own or paying on a home	
	6.3% inducted into military	
	61% qualified for or have major credit card	
	13% on welfare	
	58% employed full-time	
	28% employed part-time, etc.	

Note: This is an incomplete hypothetical example. Please also remember that the cells in the needs assessment matrix contain results statements which are measurable on an interval or ratio scale. Additionally, the items with an asterisk (*) are really outputs, not outcomes.)

Then they completed the whole form for the community and for the rest of the partners (although it was based primarily on "soft" data):

	WHAT IS		WHAT SHOULD BE
Implementers	85% certified by State DOE	100%	certified by State DOE
	79% of staff feel minorities perform equally in academic classes	90% +	feel minorities can perform in academic classes
	42% of staff feel completely competent in educational specialty, etc.	90% +	self-perceived competency, etc.
	38% "feel" schools are doing a good or better job	100%	"feel" schools are doing a good or better job
Recipients	88% "feel" all graduates should go to higher education	100%	"feel" that completers should be self-sufficient regardless of legal methods for doing so, etc.
	87% "feel" that no completers should be on welfare or convicted of crimes, etc.		

There was much discussion about the statements, including one objection to the "idealism" of the 100% figures for satisfaction and 0% on welfare rate and crime rate. The PHRD director noted that these were intended for setting goals and objectives only, and that any statement of intended results should be selected on the basis of "what is right," not on the basis of what is easily obtainable. She noted:

> If we only listed what we know we can achieve, our accomplishments would often be meager. Better that we plan on the basis of what we really want to achieve and strive for that, than "sell out" to the easy-to-achieve. And besides, we use our shortfalls for revision, not for blaming.

Then they completed the Needs Assessment matrix by supplying the rest of the "What Is" and "What Should Be" data.

After several versions and much discussion, they came to terms on the required information in the matrix. They each wrote and agreed upon the final version of the matrix, and noted that all the data they listed now dealt with outcomes. They also noted that in each subsequent version of the OEM they were developing that there were fewer inputs and processes included and more focus on results, especially outcomes.

The PHRD planning team noted that there were some shifts through the several versions of the matrix, and that there was a noticeable movement towards agreement on "what should be" as they went through the several developmental stages.

Thus was completed:

(6) Collect needs data (internal and external).

	WHAT IS	WHAT SHOULD BE
LEARNERS/ CLIENTS	63% graduated from Gotham School District. 17% of former students and completers were divorced or separated within five years. 29% of completers enrolled in higher education programs. 11% of completers were saving $1000.00 or more within five years. 43% of completers perceived their "quality of life" as average or higher as measured by . . . 11% of completers were buying their own home/ condo. within five years of completing. 61% of completers had or could qualify for major credit card. 13% of completers and dropouts were on welfare. 58% of completers and dropouts were employed full-time within six months of leaving. Etc.	100% graduated from Gotham School District. 0% of former students divorced or separated within five years. At least 59% of completers enrolled in higher education programs. At least 75% of all completers saving at least $1000.00 or more within five years of graduating. At least 90% of completers perceive their "quality of life" as average or higher as measured by. . . . At least 50% (or state average) buying their own home/condo. within five years of completing. 100% of completers could qualify for a major credit card. 0% of completers and dropouts on welfare. At least 94% of all completers and dropouts who want to be employed full-time are within six months of leaving. Etc.
EDUCATORS/ IMPLEMEN- TERS	85% Certified by State DOE. 79% of staff feel minorities are capable of performing equally academically. 42% of staff feel completely competent educationally in their specialty. Etc.	Same as above, plus: 100% of staff should be qualified for assigned duty as reported by next accrediting report. 100% of staff feel minorities are capable of equal academic perfor- mance. At least 90% of staff feel com- pletely competent in their educational specialty. Etc.
SOCIETY/ COMMUNITY	38% of the community feel that the schools are doing a good job or better. 88% of the community feel that graduates should go on to higher education. 87% of the community feel that no completer should go on welfare. . . . Etc.	Same as Learners/Clients plus: 100% of the community feels that the schools are doing a good or better job. 100% of the community feel that completers should be self-sufficient within legal means. Etc.

Figure 8.3. A partial needs assessment matrix which was accomplished by the plan- ning partners at Gotham School District. Note that the implementers included some of the professional staff concerns even though they were not Outcomes. (This is an ex- ample, and is shown only for illustrative purposes.)

Then all the partner groups met together, and came to agreement on all of the needs. Part of this "negotiating" time was spent on the issue (they called it a "need" but it wasn't) of "learner-oriented" control of the curriculum. After some discussion, the PHRD representatives realized that this issue would be unimportant if they all agreed upon the outcomes, outputs and products for Gotham School District. They entered their "what is" and "what should be" results in their OEM "score card" (Figure 8.4).

The following step was now completed:

(7) List identified and documented needs.

Then they had the next tasks of placing the needs in priority order and then listing problems for resolution.

The planning team met and each partner group sorted out the needs each had identified on the basis of two categories:

- What does it cost to meet the need?
- What does it cost to ignore the need?

Remembering that a problem was a need to be reduced or eliminated, the partners reviewed the gaps which were documented for each of the organizational elements, and then went about selecting the most important needs. There were some confusion and disagreements over which gaps were really highest priority and how to maintain and continue that which was functional (and not interfere with it). To resolve this issue they noted appropriate procedures for each of the organizational elements requiring change, plus those that should be left alone, or continued.

They produced this analysis (Figure 8.5) which was based upon the previous work and the resulting data (as shown in Figure 8.4).

After completing this form, the planning partners discussed those needs which were most important, noted all the gaps (both in results as well as those related to inputs and processes) and came to agreement. they noticed that agreement was easier this time. The educators on the PHRD team conjectured that this agreement was probably due to the facts that (1) they had agreed on outputs and outcomes first, and thus they did not have arguments over organizational efforts, and (2) they had learned to work together and were all relating means and ends through a common frame of reference.

Now, two more steps were completed:

(8) Place needs in priority order.

(9) List and obtain agreement on problems to be resolved.

They were ready for the actual system planning, for they had derived

	INPUTS	PROCESSES	PRODUCTS	OUTPUTS	OUTCOMES
WHAT IS	Annual Budget: 6.1 million 312 teachers Public Laws Board Policies Existing buildings etc.	K-12 curriculum Special Education Programs for X lrnrs. Reading clinics Educational TV available in twelve schools	Course completion rate of 88% 78% re-doers complete courses Validated reading curriculum materials etc.	63% graduated 29% enrolled in higher education 56% complete Vo-tech certificate etc.	17% divorced 61% qualified for major credit card 13% on welfare etc.
WHAT SHOULD BE	Annual Budget of 5.9 million after 5 years, 295 teachers Revised Policy, etc.	Use of validated learning techniques and materials on all learners, etc.	Course completion rate of 100% Validated reading materials, etc.	100% graduated 29% or better enrolled in higher education 100% Vo-tech certification, etc.	0% divorced 90% perceived good quality of life 100% qualified for major credit card, etc.

Figure 8.4. A *partial* OEM filled out by the planning partners at Gotham School District. Note that not all organizational elements display gaps—some things are satisfactory and require no change.

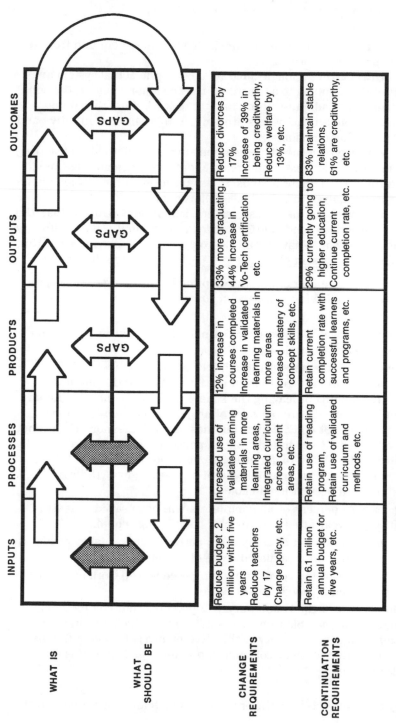

	INPUTS	PROCESSES	PRODUCTS	OUTPUTS	OUTCOMES
CHANGE REQUIREMENTS	Reduce budget .2 million within five years Reduce teachers by 17 Change policy, etc.	Increased use of validated learning materials in more learning areas, Integrated curriculum across content areas, etc.	12% increase in courses completed Increase in validated learning materials in more areas Increased mastery of concept skills, etc.	33% more graduating. 44% increase in Vo-Tech certification etc.	Reduce divorces by 17% Increase of 39% in being creditworthy, Reduce welfare by 13%, etc.
CONTINUATION REQUIREMENTS	Retain 6.1 million annual budget for five years, etc.	Retain use of reading program, Retain use of validated curriculum and methods, etc.	Retain current completion rate with successful learners and programs, etc.	29% currently going to higher education, Continue current completion rate, etc.	83% maintain stable relations, 61% are creditworthy, etc.

Figure 8.5. The partners at Gotham School District identified the above change and maintenance requirements. (Again, this is only a partial example for typifying a possible actual analysis.)

the data base for further work from a Needs Assessment and from setting the problem priorities.

The PHRD partner team decided to allocate the actual system analysis part of the planning to a subgroup: the freshman student, the councilwoman and an administrator. They got to work. First they noted that they had to convert the need statements into a Mission Objective and Performance Requirements.

They reviewed the needs assessment and the methods for setting problem priorities. Next, they read about system planning, and reviewed the system analysis steps, tools and formats for mission analysis, function analysis and methods-means analysis.

They reviewed the needs assessment matrix and realized that the mission objectives and performance requirements were directly derivable from the What-Should-Be column of the matrix. From this, they wrote the mission objective and performance requirements:

On or before five years from the adoption by the board of this mission objective, the following will have occurred:

(a) Annual budget reduced from 6.1 million per year to 5.9 million in actual dollars, regardless of inflation.

(b) Increase to 100 percent the number of graduates who (1) go on to higher education or further education, (2) get and keep jobs within five months of leaving the school program (either by graduation, or dropout), (3) are not on welfare, unemployment, or food stamps, (4) are not convicted of felonies or misdemeanors, (5) are not divorced or legally separated from a spouse, (6) are able to get credit as indicated by ability to get at least one major credit card, (7) are wanting to seek full-time employment and get a job of their first, second or third occupational choice.

(c) At least 75 percent of all completers will have saved at least $1,000.00 per year after five years of completing school.

(d) At least 90 percent of completers perceive their quality of life as "good" or better on a validated scale of Quality of Life.

(e) 100 percent of the community will perceive the Gotham School District as doing a "good" job or better.

(f) 100 percent of the community will perceive that completers and dropouts should be able to be self-sufficient, self-reliant, and contributing members of society within five months of leaving the district as indicated by their consumption being equal to or less than their production.

They reviewed this with the entire planning team, and noted that the subgroup's work had met all the requirements: listing only outcomes (societal impact results) and all objectives were in fact measurable on an interval or ratio scale. The mission objective and performance requirements were adopted, and then the subgroup went on to develop a mission profile for getting from where the school district was now to the point where they would meet the mission objective and its performance requirements. After some midnight oil (it was their first system planning experience) they came back with the mission profile for review (Figure 8.6).

The total planning team reviewed it, and generally approved. There were some disagreements about some of the functions, so the subgroup decided that they really did have to write performance requirements for each function in the mission profile. They went away and returned with it. Figure 8.7 lists the performance requirements they derived for Functions 1.0 and 2.0.

After reviewing the mission profile along with the performance requirements, the confusion about what each function meant was cleared up. The team made some minor corrections to the mission profile, and moved to the next task, which was to perform the function analysis—to develop "break-outs" of each of the functions in the mission profile.

The function analyses were completed for all of the functions in the mission profile (the function analyses of 1.0 and 3.0 are presented in Figures 8.8 and 8.9).

All of the lower-level functions (which came from each of the functions in the mission profile) were then broken down into their constituent functions. In addition, each time there was a function identified, the performance requirements for each were derived and presented in the same way as for the performance requirements for the Mission Profile (see Figure 8.6).

The mission and function analyses along with the performance requirements were brought back to the planning partners, and after some modifications, were approved.

It was now time to complete the methods-means analysis. The PHRD group noted that it was important to identify that which had to be changed as well as that which was working well enough to continue. They checked back with the OEM form that they had developed (Figure 8.4) and added another set of dimensions to it:

- the identified possible interventions (or methods-means) for each of the performance requirements (or families of requirements)
- the selected interventions

The OEM "job-aid" was completed and served as an overall guide,

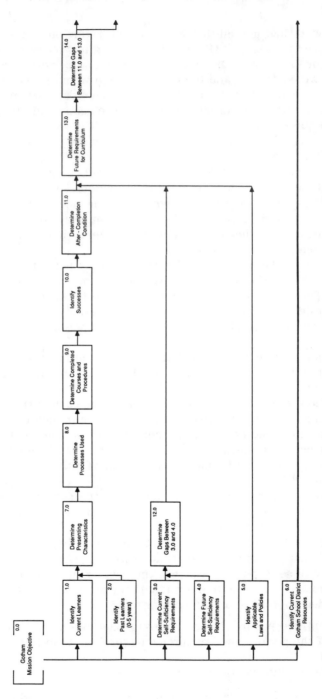

Figure 8.6 (left). The mission profile for meeting the Gotham School District mission objective and performance requirements. Note that included in this mission profile are all six steps of the generic problem-solving process.

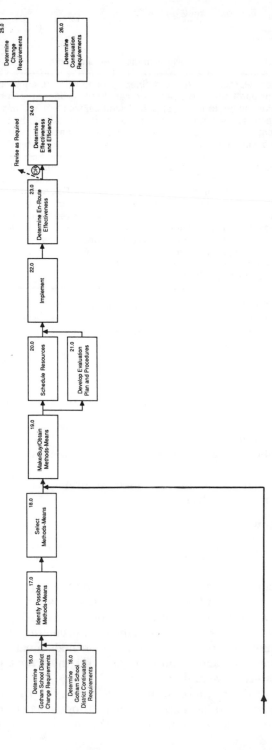

Figure 8.6 (right). The mission profile for meeting the Gotham School District mission objective and performance requirements. Note that included in this mission profile are all six steps of the generic problem-solving process.

Function Number	Performance Requirements
1.0	Current learners are those defined as ones who are enrolled currently at full- or part-time, who qualify for state funding under the current state regulations on financing of public schools; who are in a regular or special program within Gotham School District as defined by Board of Education Policies 37.8, 43.11 and 45.2 and those in cooperative programs with other educational agencies as defined under Policy 13.3.
2.0	Self-sufficiency is defined as the level where an individual's consumption is equal to or less than her/his production. The exact criteria for self-sufficiency will be approved by Professor Fox of State University as being a valid indicator, on or before October 1 of this year. The current level of self-sufficiency in Gotham will be derived from the criteria, and the resulting self-sufficiency for Gotham will include the greater metropolitan area as bounded by the City Council Master Plan of October 13, 1989, or the latest Master Plan available. This Gotham level of current self-sufficiency will be approved by Professor Fox as valid on or before January 15th of next year.

Figure 8.7. Two of the performance requirements that were developed by the Gotham PHRD subgroup. These give the criteria by which one could determine if each of the functions was accomplished, and if they were accomplished correctly. (Only two performance requirements are presented here.)

which would serve as the methods-means analysis. Thus, they had completed:

- needs assessment
- mission objective and performance requirements
- mission profile
- function analysis and performance requirements
- methods-means analysis

Completed now:

(10) Determine mission, functions and performance requirements and identify possible methods-means.

The planning team was ready for reconciling the constraints.

The methods-means had been identified in such a way so that there were at least two possible sets of interventions for every performance requirement or "families" of performance requirements (when several of them naturally went together). For each methods-means there were listed the advantages and disadvantages, and their next job was to select the most effective and efficient.

During the analysis, there were some "sticky" places where it seemed as if there were no solutions (or methods-means) for meeting some of the performance requirements. For instance, scheduling the

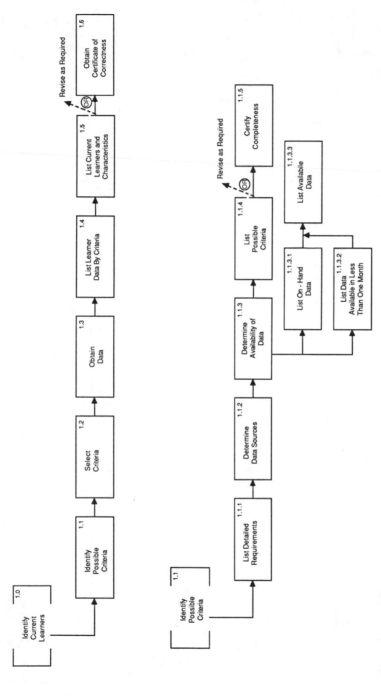

Figure 8.8. The function analysis (first level and a sample second level) of Function 1.0 of the Gotham School District mission profile. Note that each function could be broken down at least one and usually several levels more.

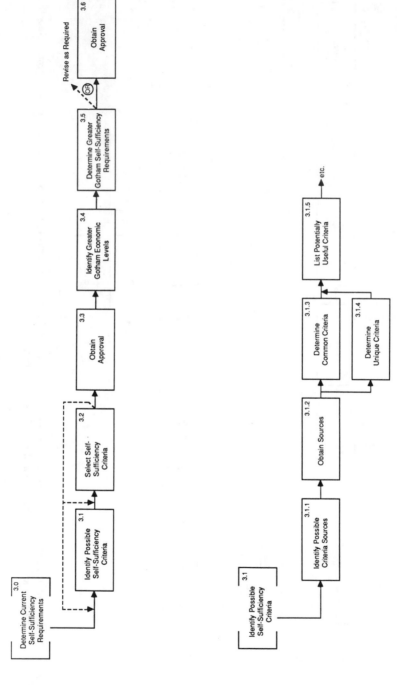

Figure 8.9. The function analysis (first level and an example of a second level) of Function 3.0 of the Gotham School District mission profile. Each function here could be broken down into several lower levels of function analysis.

classrooms for non-regular special student-teacher activities utilizing the existing policy of "first scheduled, first used" was in conflict with another policy that "emergencies come first." It seemed that there were a few old-timers around the District who always wanted to schedule their activities as "emergencies" so that they could have the best times for themselves (and have their schedules as convenient as possible). So something new had to be "invented" so that emergency scheduling was really for emergencies only. A possible methods-means was invented whereby a new policy was derived to cover this: an "emergency" activity requiring one activity to supersede another previously scheduled activity had to be approved by the two faculty involved, never by an outside staff member. This would cut down on any "bullying" of a schedule by a self-seeking or inconsiderate person.

Other constraints were eliminated in this same manner, and thus they completed:

(11) Reconcile any constraints.

The PHRD planning team met. They had been sharing their progress with their constituents, and most reported that they were pleased with both the progress of the planning, the prospects for the future, and the growing acceptance of the purposes of planning and expectations for the future. Now they had to actually select the methods-means.

In order to make their selection, the team invited a systems analyst to advise them about the relationships between costs and results. They had noted some questions about options, and the consultant, along with the director of PHRD, had done some studies, including a simulation of what would happen if several of the methods-means were chosen.

Based upon cost-results analyses (what results will you get as compared to the costs of achieving the results), the possible selections were evaluated. The simulation data were later useful on some of the choices, since there were contingencies which had been "tried out on paper" before choosing.

The alternative solutions were selected, and listed. The entire list of performance requirements, the solutions (methods-means) chosen along with the implementation plan (Function 22.0 of Figure 8.6) were given to the superintendent and board for approval. They were generally pleased. However, the board wondered about the actual evaluation of this whole plan, and asked for clarification on how the program would be monitored. Quickly, the director of PHRD produced the evaluation plan (Function 21.0, Figure 8.6) and after careful review, the plan was approved by the board. Thus was completed:

(12) Select methods-means.

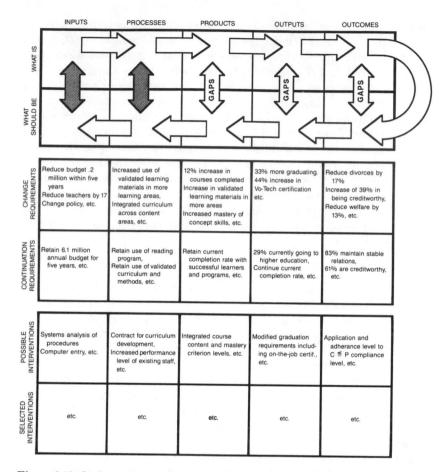

Figure 8.10. Linking problem solving and planning to needs assessment information through identifying change and continuation requirements, possible interventions, and selected interventions which will change what should be changed and continue that which is currently successful.

Now the action began. A master program schedule was constructed which displayed the functions and subfunctions to be performed, along with assessment criteria in order to identify when each was to be performed and completed. A plan for completion of each function, including delivery of hardware and equipment as well as in-service training and staff development, was developed and scheduled. New policies were drawn up, signed, posted, and discussed. New procedures were implemented, and a minimum of confusion resulted due to careful explanations. A few times when conflict came about (the classroom scheduling again), there were firm and rational policies which the deputy superintendent was able to communicate with a minimum of hard feelings. The implementation plan and schedule were constantly checked, and few things went wrong.

Completed now was:

(13) Implement methods-means.

During the implementation, some things did not work out, and revisions were required. Because there were performance requirements for each function, it was a simple matter to formatively evaluate during this implementation in order to identify what was right, what was wrong, and thus what to change.

For each function and its associated peformance requirements, the PHRD planning team—now renamed the Implementation Team—after adding three district staff members and dropping off the councilwoman, listed that which was working well, and that which had to be revised.

Completed now:

(14) Determine en-route effectiveness.

They listed alternative methods-means to correct the failures, developed a plan for each, based upon another methods-means analysis, and made recommendations to the Board on the "stickier" ones, and got approvals for the changes.

The changes were made, and some new procedures were implemented. One which had to be changed was the reward system for teachers whose learners mastered material and concepts more quickly than the previous average. The faculty union, which represented many of the educators, refused to cooperate in giving approval for financial incentives to quickly-performing learners and their teachers. The staff of Gotham School District had to meet with the regional director of the union to get some changes in their policy.

Because of such restraints, the system plan only worked partially, so the Gotham School District plan had to be revised. After making the changes, the implementation continued, and progress was constantly monitored, and changes made as required:

(15) Revise as (and if) required.

The plan and methods-means continued to operate, and it was time for a program assessment at the first major summative evaluation period (after two years).

Two dimensions were evaluated:

- effectiveness of the total plan and all of its parts
- efficiency of the total plan and all of its parts

Each of the performance requirements for the mission objective was subjected to detailed evaluation. What had worked, what had not, and how did the total plan of Gotham School District work relative to meeting the mission objective?

An evaluation team was set up, and results were compared to objectives. Each function and set of performance requirements were evaluated in terms of which had been accomplished, and which were worth accomplishing in terms of expended time, effort and resources.

Some data were missing, and again they commissioned an external study to determine the societal/community impact.

All of the data were in, and the PHRD Implementation Team (formerly the planning team) met and reviewed the data:

(16) Determine educational system(s') effectiveness and efficiency.

Based on the summative evaluation data the Implementation Team was ready to make some recommendations. But first, they asked for some observational (soft data) reports from people both within and outside of the system who had not been part of either the planning or the evaluation. They shared with the team that which they saw as going correctly, and some unexpected things (such as a growing public awareness by some of the community that the district was "getting its act together," and some thought the food for students and staff in the cafeteria was even reasonably good now). This informal review of unplanned results (goal-free evaluation) was added to the effectiveness and efficiency (summative) results. Now completed was:

(17) Determine revision and continuation requirements.

Now for the recommendations.

The PHRD Implementation Team listed those things which should be changed, and those which were working well enough to continue. For instance, the pre-graduation counseling program seemed to be a major force in quicker self-sufficiency after completing high school, but the home counseling function seemed not to be realizing its potential. Some changes in the home counseling procedures were recommended.

All of the recommendations for change and continuation were completed and given to the superintendent and the board. They met, thought that the recommendations were worthy, commended the team on being "scientific," and approved the revisions and the continuation of the plan.

The "last" step was completed—for now, since the entire process is an ongoing one:

(18) Implement changes while continuing the entire process.

The board even "institutionalized" the process, and called for a

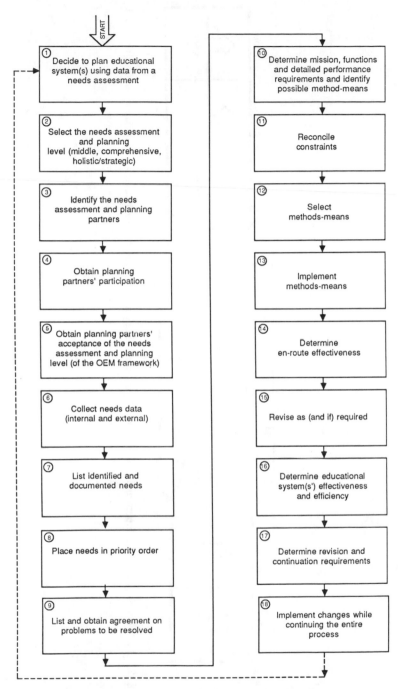

Figure 8.11. Eighteen steps for planning educational systems.

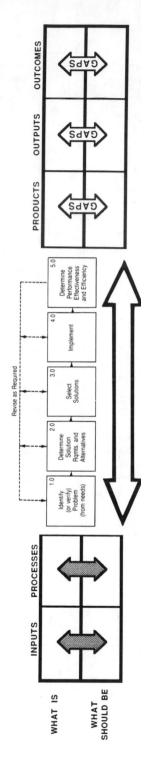

Figure 8.12. The "what should be's" of inputs and processes may be seen as being derived, through system analysis, from the balance of the OEM.

repeat every two years of the entire needs assessment, system planning, selection, implementation, evaluation, and revision cycle. They believe that this process would indeed allow them, on a continuing basis, to develop an ongoing strategic plan to define and achieve "excellence."

The Gotham School District "story" got around national circles, and more and more people visited the program. The PHRD staff at Gotham first started giving seminars at regional meetings, and then, under contract, started training staff members of other districts.

The news about needs assessment and system planning was getting around, and getting accepted. It worked, and others wanted "in" on the process.

★ ★ ★ ★ ★

an eighteen-step process for a system approach to education

The eighteen steps of a system approach which are specific to the planning of educational systems are shown in Figure 8.11.

When designing, developing, and implementing a system approach to education, the planner should go through each of the eighteen steps:

- Steps 1 through 9 deal with needs assessment.
- Steps 10–15 relate to the system analysis and implementation of that which is being planned.
- Steps 16–18 are concerned with summative evaluation and revision of the entire educational system.

The OEM may be used as a "job aid"—a template, or pattern—which will allow one to identify all of the pieces and actions of an educational system. If one wishes to fill out the OEM by using it as a "score card" with which to keep track of planning and progress, it should be noted that the processes and inputs elements of "what should be" may be filled in after doing the system analysis (see Figure 8.12).

The concepts, tools, techniques, and methods provided by a system approach to education should allow the planning of educational systems which will yield measurably improved results. Our futures just might depend upon it.

BIBLIOGRAPHY

ALKIN, M. C. and J. E. BRUNO. "System Approaches to Educational Planning," Part IV of *Social and Technological Change: Implications for Education.* Eugene, OR:ERIC/CEA (1970).

ASTIN, A. W. and R. J. PANOS. "The Evaluation of Education Programs," in *Educational Measurement* (2nd ed.). R. L. Thorndike, ed. Washington, D.C.:American Council on Education (1971).

AYRES, R. U. *Technological Forecasting and Long-Range Planning.* New York: McGraw-Hill (1969).

BAKER, E. L. *Evaluating Instructional Programs.* Los Angeles:University of California (April, 1974).

BANGHART, F. W. *Educational Systems Analysis.* Toronto, Ontario:TheMacMillan Co. (1969).

BELL, R. and J. COPLANS. *Decisions, Decisions: Game Theory and You.* New York: W. W. Norton (1976).

BERTALANFFY, L. VON. *General Systems Theory.* New York:George Braziller (1968).

BRANSON, R. K., et al. Interservice procedures for instructional systems development (Phases I, II, III, IV, V, and Executive Summary. U.S. Army Training and Doctrine Command Pamphlet 350.) Fort Monroe, VA (August, 1975).

BRIGGS, L. J. (ed.). *Instructional Design: Principles and Applications.* Englewood Cliffs, NJ:Educational Technology Publications (1977).

BRIGGS, L. J. and W. W. WAGER. *Handbook of Procedures for the Design of Instruction* (2nd ed.). Englewood Cliffs, NJ:Educational Technology Publications.

BUCKLEY, W. (ed.). *Modern Systems Research for the Behavioral Scientist.* Chicago, IL: Aldine Publishing Company (1968).

BUTZ, R. "En-Route Social Indicators," *Performance & Instruction Journal,* 22(8): 28–31.

"Can Corporate America Cope?" *Newsweek.* Quotation of H. Ross Perot (November 17, 1986).

CARTER, L. F. *The Systems Approach to Education—The Mystique and the Reality.* System Development Corporation, Report SP-3921 (1969).

CARTER, R. K. *The Accountable Agency* (Human Service Guide No. 34). Beverly Hills: Sage Publications (1983).

CHURCHMAN, C. W. *The Systems Approach* (1st and 2nd eds.). New York:Dell Publishing Company (1969, 1975).

CLELAND, D. I. and W. R. KING. *Systems Analysis and Project Management.* New York:McGraw-Hill Company (1968).

CLELAND, D. I. and W. R. KING. *Systems, Organizations, Analysis, Management: A Book of Readings.* New York:McGraw-Hill Book Company (1969).

COOK, D. L. *PERT: Applications in Education* (OE-1214, Cooperative Research Monograph No. 17). Washington, D.C.:U.S. Government Printing Office (1966).

COOLEY, W. W. *Methods of Evaluating School Innovations.* Pittsburgh: University of Pittsburgh, Learning and Research and Development Center (1971).

COOLEY, W. W. and W. E. BICKEL. *Decision-Oriented Educational Research.* Boston: Klluwer-Nijhoff Publishing (1986).

CORRIGAN, R. E., et al. *A System Approach for Education (SAFE).* Garden Grove, CA: R. E. Corrigan Associates (1975).

CORRIGAN, R. E. and BETTY O. CORRIGAN. *SAFE: System Approach for Effectiveness.* Anaheim, CA:R. E. Corrigan Associates (1985).

CORRIGAN, R. E. and R. KAUFMAN. *Why System Engineering?* Palo Alto, CA:Fearon Publishers (1966).

CORRIGAN, R. E., R. A. KAUFMAN, BETTY O. CORRIGAN, et al. *Operation PEP: Preparing Educational Planners.* A series of instructional and training modules prepared under ESEA Title III Funds in cooperation with the California State Department of Education, Chapman College, and Litton Industries (1967).

DICK, W. and L. CAREY. *The Systematic Design of Instruction* (2nd ed.). Glenview, IL: Scott Foresman & Co. (1985).

DRUCKER, P. F. *Management: Tasks, Responsibilities, Practices.* New York:Harper & Row (1973).

DRUCKER, P. F. *Innovation and Entrepreneurship.* London:William Heinemann, Ltd. (1985).

Educational Testing Service. Highlights of a report from Educational Testing Service to the State Board of Education of the Commonwealth of Pennsylvania: A Plan for evaluating the quality of educational programs in Pennsylvania, Princeton, NJ (June, 1965).

FINN, C. E., JR. *What Works: Research About Teaching and Learning.* Washington, D.C.:U.S. Department of Education (1986).

FRANKL, V. *Man's Search for Meaning: An Introduction to Logo-Therapy.* Boston: Beacon Press (1962).

Gagne, R. M. *Psychological Principles in System Development.* New York:Holt, Rinehart & Wilson (1962).

GAGNE, R. M. *The Conditions of Learning* (4th ed.). New York:Holt, Rinehart & Winston (1985).

GAGNE, R. M. and L. J. BRIGGS. *Principles of Instructional Design* (2nd ed.). New York:Holt, Rinehart & Winston (1979).

GILBERT, T. F. "Mathetics: The Technology of Education," in *Instructional Design: Readings.* M. D. Merrill, ed. Englewood Cliffs, NJ:Prentice-Hall (1971).

GLASER, R. Psychological bases for instructional design, *AV Communication Review* (Winter, 1966).

GREENWALD, H. and E. RICH. *The Happy Person: A Seven Step Plan.* New York:Avon Books (1984).

HERSEY, P. and K. BLANCHARD. *Management of Organizational Behavior: Utilizing Human Resources* (4th ed.). Englewood, Cliffs, NJ:Prentice-Hall, Inc. (1982).

HODGKINSON, H. L. *All One System: Demographics of Education, Kindergarten Through Graduate School.* Washington, D.C.:Institute for Educational Leadership, Inc. (1985).

HODGKINSON, H. L. "Reform? Higher Education? Don't Be Absurd!" *Phi Delta Kappan,* 68(4) (December, 1986).

HOUSE, E. R. and R. L. LINNE. Review of "Losing Ground: American Social Policy 1950–1980," *Educational Evaluation and Policy Analysis*, 8(3) (Fall, 1986).

ISAAC, S. and W. B. MICHAEL. *Handbook in Research and Evaluation*. San Diego, CA:Knapp (1971).

KANTER, R. M. *The Change Masters: Innovation & Entrepreneurship in the American Corporation*. New York:Simon & Schuster (1983).

KAUFMAN, R. A. "A System Approach to Education—Derivation and Definition," *AV Communication Review*, 16:415–425 (1968).

KAUFMAN, R. A. "A Possible Integrative Model for the Systematic and Measurable Improvement of Education," *American Psychologist*, 26(3):250–256 (1971).

KAUFMAN, R. A. *Educational System Planning*. Englewood Cliffs, NJ:Prentice-Hall, Inc. (1972).

KAUFMAN, R. "Determining and Diagnosing Organizational Needs," *Group and Organizational Studies*, 6(3):312–322 (1981).

KAUFMAN, R. *Identifying and Solving Problems: A System Approach* (3rd ed.). San Diego, CA:University Associates Publishers (1982).

KAUFMAN, R. "A Holistic Planning Model: A System Approach for Improving Organizational Effectiveness and Impact," *Performance & Instruction Journal*, 22(8):3–12 (1983a).

KAUFMAN, R. "Planning and Organizational Improvement Terms," *Performance & Instruction Journal*, 22(8):12–15 (1983b).

KAUFMAN, R. "Improving Organizational Impact: A Western Alternative to Japanese Management," *Performance & Instruction Journal*, 23(8):11–15 (1984).

KAUFMAN, R. "Linking Training to Organizational Impact," *Journal of Instructional Development*, 8(2):23–29 (1985).

KAUFMAN, R. "Assessing Needs," in *Introduction to Performance Technology*. M. Smith, ed. Washington, D.C.:The National Society for Performance and Instruction (1986).

KAUFMAN, R. "Obtaining Functional Results: Relating Needs Assessment, Needs Analysis, and Objectives," *Educational Technology*, 26(1):24–27 (1986a).

KAUFMAN, R. "An Algorithm for Identifying and Allocating Performance Problems," *Performance & Instruction Journal*, 25(1):21 (1986b).

KAUFMAN, R. "A Needs Assessment Primer," *Training and Development Journal* (Oct., 1987).

KAUFMAN, R. *Guia Practica Para la Planeacion en las Organizaciones*. Mexico City:Editorial Trillas (1987a).

KAUFMAN R. and A. S. CARRON. "Utility and Self-Sufficiency in the Selection of Educational Alternatives," *Journal of Instructional Development*, 4(1):14–18, 23–26 (1980).

KAUFMAN, R. A., R. E. CORRIGAN and D. W. JOHNSON. "Towards Educational Responsiveness to Society's Needs: A Tentative Utility Model," *Journal of Socio-Economic Planning Sciences*, 3:151–157 (1969).

KAUFMAN, R. and F. W. ENGLISH. *Needs Assessment: Concept and Application*. Englewood Cliffs, NJ:Educational Technology Publishers (1979).

KAUFMAN, R., R. G. STAKENAS, J. C. WAGER and H. MAYER. "Relating Needs Assessment, Program Development, Implementation and Evaluation," *Journal of Instructional Development*, 4(4):17–26 (1981).

KAUFMAN, R. and B. STONE. *Planning for Organizational Success: A Practical Guide*. New York:John Wiley and Sons, Inc., Business Series (1983).

KAUFMAN, R. and S. THIAGARAJAN. "Identifying and Specifying Requirements for Instruction: Concepts and Application," in *Instructional Technology*. R. Gagne, ed. Lawrence Erlbaum Associates, Inc. (1987).

KAUFMAN, R. and SUSAN THOMAS. *Evaluation Without Fear*. New York:New Viewpoints Division, Franklin Watts, Inc. (1980).

KOMISAR, B. P. "'Need' and the Needs-Curriculum," in *Language and Concepts in Education*. B. O. Smith and R. H. Ennis, eds. Chicago:Rand McNally & Co. (1961).

LASWELL, H. D. *The Communication of Ideas*. New York:Harper & Row (1948).

LESSINGER, L. M. *Every Kid A Winner*. New York:Simon & Schuster (1970).

LEVIN, H. M. *Cost Effectiveness: A Primer* (New perspectives in evaluation). Beverly Hills:Sage Publications (1983).

MAGER, R. F. *Preparing Instructional Objectives* (2nd ed). Belmont, CA:Pitman Learning, Inc. (1975).

MAGER, R. F. *Making Instruction Work: Or Skillbloomers*. Belmont, CA:David S. Lake Publishers (1988).

MAGER, R. F. and K. M. BEACH, JR. *Developing Vocational Instruction*. Palo Alto:Fearon Publishers, Inc. (1967).

MARTINO, J. P. *Technological Forecasting for Decision-Making* (2nd ed.) New York: North-Holland (1983).

MASLOW, A. *Motivation and Personality*. New York:Harper & Row (1954).

MAYER, N. (ed.). *GAIA: An Atlas of Planet Management*. New York:Anchor Books (1984).

MEALS, D. "Heuristic Models for Systems Planning," *Phi Delta Kappan*, Bloomington, Indiana (January 1967).

MERRILL, M. D. "Component Display Theory," in *Instructional Design Theories and Models: An Overview of the Current Status*. Hillsdale, NJ:Lawrence Erlbaum Associates (1983).

MORGAN, R. M. and C. B. CHADWICK. *Systems Analysis for Educational Change: The Republic of Korea*. Tallahassee:Florida State University, Department of Educational Research (1971).

MURRAY, C. *Losing Ground: American Social Policy 1950–1980*. New York:Basic Books (1984).

PASCALE, R. T. and A. G. ATHOS. *The Art of Japanese Management: Applications for American Executives*. New York:Warner Books, Inc. (1981).

PEDDIWELL, J. A. (H. Benjamin). *The Sabertooth Curriculum*. New York:McGraw-Hill (1939).

PETERS, T. *Thriving on Chaos: Handbook for a Management Revolution*. New York:Alfred A. Knopf (1987).

PETERS, T. J. and N. AUSTIN. *The Passion for Excellence: The Leadership Difference*. New York:Random House (1985).

PETERS, T. J. and R. H. WATERMAN, JR. *In Search of Excellence: Lessons Learned from America's Best Run Companies*. New York:Harper & Row (1982).

Phi Delta Kappa. *Handbook for Conducting Future Studies in Education*. Bloomington, Indiana:Phi Delta Kappa (1984).

POPHAM, W. J. *Educational Objectives*. Los Angeles:Vimcet Associates (1966).

POPHAM, W. J. (ed.). *Evaluation in Education*. Berkeley, CA:McCutchan (1974).

POPHAM, W. J. and T. R. HUSEK. "Implications of Criterion-Referenced Measurement," *Journal of Educational Measurement*, 6 (1969).

RAPPAPORT, A. *General System Theory*. Cambridge, MA:Abacus Press (1986).

REIGELUTH, C. M. (ed.) *Instructional Design Theories and Models: An Overview of the Current Status*. Hillsdale, NJ:Lawrence Erlbaum Associates (1983).

ROGERS, C. "Toward a Modern Approach to Values: The Valuing Process in the Mature Person," *The Journal of Abnormal and Social Psychology*, 68(2) (1964).

SCHAAF, M. "Wants: Whether We Need Them or Not," *Los Angeles Times*, Part V, p. 3 (October 24, 1986).

SCRIVEN, M. "The Methodology of Evaluation," in *Perspective of Curriculum Evaluation*. R. Tyler, R. M. Gagne and M. Scriven. (AERA Monograph Series on Curriculum Evaluation). Chicago:Rand McNally & Co. (1967).

SCRIVEN, M. "Goal Free Evaluation," in *School Evaluation: The Politics and Process*. E. R. House, ed. Berkeley, CA:McCutchan (1973).

SILVERN, L. C. "Cybernetics and Education K-12," *Audiovisual Instruction* (March, 1968).

STAKENAS, R. G. and D. B. MOCK. "Context Evaluation: The Use of History in Policy Analysis," *The Public Historian*, 17(3) (1985).

STUFFLEBEAM, D. L., W. J. FOLEY, W. R. GEPHART, R. L. HAMMON, H. O. MERRIMAN and M. M. PROVUS. *Educational Evaluation and Decision Making*. Itasca, IL:Peacock (1971).

TOFFLER, A. *Future Shock*. New York:Random House (1970).

TOFFLER, A. *The Third Wave*. New York:Morrow (1980).

WITKIN, B. R. *Assessing Needs in Educational and Social Programs*. San Francisco: Jossey-Bass (1984).

INDEX

accountability, 38, *def.* 60
analysis, 124–125
  levels of, 36, 125
  methods of systems, 166–170
  see also system analysis, systems analysis

change, educational
  units of, 36
CLELAND, D., 166
constraint, *def.* 60
cost-results analysis, 159, *def.* 161, 195
criterion-reference item, 174
Critical Path Method (CPM), 171
cross-impact analysis, 169
curriculum, 9, 11, 29, 63, 135, 138, 149, 170
cycle analysis, 170

decision theory, 168
Delphi technique, 169
discrepancy analysis, 63, 104
DRUCKER, P., 42

educational agencies, 33, 37
educational engineering, 5
educational management, 18, 25–27, 39–40, *def.* 60
educational manager, 26, 40, 55
educational planning, 18–19
educational outcome, 72
ends, *def.* 12, 21
  in education, 12
educational system analysis, 44, 51–52, 160

process of, 45
steps in, 52
educational system design, 45
educational system planning, 18–21, *def.* 60, 91, 160, 163, 174
  eighteen-step process, 199
  partners in, 69–71
evaluation, of system plan, 171–173, 197–198
  and performance effectiveness, 172, 198
  goal-free, 174
  formative, 174
  summative, 175, 197–198
  types of, 172–173

feasibility study, 151
  and method-means analysis, 158
flow chart construction, 119–123
  and system analysis, 120
function, 48, 103, 113, 117, *def.* 145
  and mission analysis, 103–106
  compatibility among, 135
  examples of, 113–114
  identification of, 48
  interaction among, 116
  levels of, 116–118, 189–194
  parallel, 145
  series, 145
function analysis, *def.* 48, 60, 110, 113–115, 118, 131, 133–135
  and method-means analysis, 133, 135, 152–153
  and mission analysis, 133, 145
  and task analysis, 145

functional analysis *(continued)*
  example of, 126–127, 189–194
  feasibility of, 134
  flow chart of, 49, 118, 122, 129, 132
  rules for, 119
  summary of, 133–134

game theory, 168

holistic focus, 7, 31
holistic framework, 29
holistic planning, 31, 37, 178
holistic unit of analysis, 37, 68–69
human concerns, 75
humanistic theories of behavior, 75

individualization of instruction, 132,
    150
  function analysis, 132
inductive logic, 35
inputs, 29, 30, 32–33
instructional materials, analysis in
    selecting, 46–47

Japanese management, 8, 36

learning performance, 37
learning task analysis, 135

management, 60
  and education, 25, 39–40
Management by Objective (MBO), 180
methods, for systems analysis, 166–
    170
  implementation of, 197
methods-means analysis, 45, *def.* 50,
    60, 134–135, 149–161, 162
  and function analysis, 134–135; 152–
    153; 189
  flow chart of, 50, 152–153
  selection of, 165, 195
  steps in, 157
mission, *def.* 92, 96, 110–111
mission analysis, 20, 45–46, *def.* 60,
    91–92, 99–101, 106, 110, 123–125
  and function analysis, 115, 126–133,
    145
  and methods-means, analysis, 133
  and needs assessment, 123
  and task analysis, 145, 154
  diagram of, 106

elements of, 92, 110
example of, 47
steps in, 47
mission objective, 44, 46, *def.* 93, 93–
    98, 102, 110–111
  and performance data, 98–99, 101
  and performance requirements, 126
  conditions of, 96
  examples of, 126, 188
mission profile, 46, 103–109, 111, 115,
    128
  example of, 107, 108–109, 189
  expansion of, 126–133
  flowchart of, 47, 108–109, 128
  steps in, 104–105

needs, *def.* 13–14, 21, 40–41, 43, 45,
    54, 64, 70, 82
  data and, 76, 181–182
  determining, 64–67
  examples of, 43, 66, 114, 183–184
  faulty, 66–67, 80
  prioritizing of, 84, 185
needs analysis, 15, 20, 36, *def.* 21, 65–67
needs assessment, *def.* 15, 19–20, 22, 25,
    27, 36, 41, 58, 64, 77, 163
  characteristics of, 64
  data for, 42, 64, 71, 73, 76, 77–79, 101,
    181–182
  faulty types of, 65
  levels of, 67–68
  nine steps in, 64–65
  summary needs assessment matrix,
    89, 182–184
  three types of, 41
needs matrix, 80, 88
  example of, 81, 83, 183–184
needs sensing, 42, 71, 88
needs statement, 70–71
nominal group technique, 169

objective, *def.* 22, 94, 97
operational gaming, 168, 175
operations research, 166
organization results, 17, *def.* 22, 40
organizational efforts, 17, *def.* 22
Organizational Elements (OE's), 29–30,
    34, 37, *def.* 61, 181
  and organizational results, 30, 181
  number of, 29, 34
Organizational Elements Model (OEM),

29, 33–34, 37, 40, 58, *def.* 61, 164
and education, 34, 38–40, 179–181
and levels of planning, 61
and six-step problem solving, 56–57, 164
applied to education needs, 181
flow chart of, 179, 181, 186
two-tiered, 35, 61
outcome, 12, *def.* 22, 38, 39
educational, 72
output, *def.* 22, 29–30, 32–33

performance, units of (tasks), 133, 135–145
performance data, in education, 42, 78
performance objectives, 93
performance requirements, *def.* 61, 98, 135, 150–151, 171, 189, 192
and function analysis, 126, 130, 134, 192
and method-means analysis, 151
and mission objective, 98, 101, 110
and task analysis, 137, 140
criteria of, 130, 140, 192
list of, 99
table of, 100
PEROT, H. ROSS, 33
plan, *def.* 22, 170–171
planning, *def.* 2, 8, 27, 65
and needs assessment, 65–67
and educational systems, 18, 20, 21
levels of, 16, 29–33, 41, 67–68
partners in, 69, 75–76
planning domains, 32
planning-programming budgeting system, 167
polling, 169
problem, 15, *def.* 22, 61, 63, 85, 87
problem resolution, 52, 85–86
problem solving, 25–163
and OE, 56–57
and system analysis, 52
flow chart of, 48
six-step process, 18, 27, 56–58, *def.* 61, 164, 190–191
processes, 29–30, 33
products, 29, 30, 32–35, 119
and mission profile, 107
Program Evaluation Review Technique (PERT), 5, 171, *def.* 175

quality of life factors, 41, *def.* 61, 74, 88
quasi-need, 80
quasi-needs assessment, 17, 77
queuing, 168

reading skills, 149–150
relevance trees, 168
results, 13, *def.* 61, 70, 93, 111
and performance objectives as function, 103–104, 115
classification of, 111
measuring of, 103
results chain, 33, 37–38, 76, 97
revision, of system/plan/design, 54, 173–198
and evaluation, 173

self-sufficiency factors, 41–42, *def.* 43, 61, 72, 74, 88
collecting data on, 79
specified in terms of money, 72
simulation, 53, *def.* 175
and systems analysis, 167
societal consequences of planning, *def.* 17, 22, 72
societal indicators, 35
society, 70
system, 12, *def.* 22
system analysis, *def.* 16, 20, 44, 50, 55–56, 61, 91, 163–164, 188
educational, 51–52, 54
example of, 50, 51, 151
flowcharts in, 120, 131
levels of, 123
how to end, 135
summary of, 51, 56
system approach, 1, *def.* 15, 16, 22, 54–56, 59
applied to education, 28–31, 54, 201
eighteen-step process, 201
summary of, 56, 58–59
system concepts, 5, *def.* 12, 22
system models, 6
and systems models, 6
system performance, 53
system revision, 53–54
see also revision
system synthesis, 59
systematic approach, *see* system approach.

systems analysis, 165–166, *def.* 175
    techniques of, 166–170, 175
systems approaches, 5–7, *def.* 22
systems models, 6

task, 133, 135–145
    derivation of, 136
task analysis, 133, 135–145
    relation to function, mission analysis,

    136, 144–145
    steps in, 137
task description, 139–144
    chart of, 142–143
    steps in, 140–141
task listing, 137–138
TOFFLER, A., 2, 4

want, 89

ABOUT THE AUTHOR

ROGER KAUFMAN IS professor and director of the Center for Needs Assessment and Planning, The Florida State University. He received his M.A. from Johns Hopkins University and his Ph.D. from New York University. Previously he was an assistant to the Vice President for Engineering at Douglas Aircraft Company and a professor at United States International University and Chapman College. Dr. Kaufman is the author of more than fifteen books and over eighty journal articles in psychology and education. He has served as president of the National Society for Performance and Instruction (NSPI); as consultant to the U.S. Secretary of Health, Education, and Welfare; as a member of the Secretary of the Navy's Advisory Board on Education and Training; on the Education Committee of the United States Chamber of Commerce; and is a consultant to many educational, industrial, and military organizations, both nationally as well as in Australia, Central and South America, and Europe. He was the 1983 Haydn Williams Fellow at the Western Australian Institute of Technology (now the Curtin University of Technology). He is a Fellow of the American Psychological Association (Educational Psychology) and a Diplomate of the American Board of Psychology (School Psychology).

371.207
K21

7812

LINCOLN CHRISTIAN COLLEGE AND SEMINARY